Nothing But the Blood

BAILEY E. SMITH

NOTHING
BUT THE
BLOOD

BROADMAN PRESS
Nashville, Tennessee

ISBN: 0-8054-1537-8
Dewey Decimal Classification: 252
Subject Headings: SERMONS - COLLECTED WORKS
Library of Congress Catalog Card Number: 86-23325
Printed in the United States of America

Unless otherwise indicated, all Scripture quotations are from the King James Version of the Bible.

Library of Congress Cataloging-in-Publication Data

Smith, Bailey E.
 Nothing but the blood.

 1. Atonement—Sermons. 2. Jesus Christ—Crucifixion—Sermons. 3. Satisfaction for sin—Sermons. 4. Southern Baptist Convention—Sermons. 5. Baptists—Sermons. 6. Sermons, American. I. Title.
BT265.2.S64 1987   232′.3   86-23325
ISBN 0-8054-1537-8 (pbk.)

This book
is dedicated
to Don
&
Sue
Lucky
cherished loved ones
and dear friends
and to their children
Donnie and Toni and
my brothers and sister
Danny, Bobby, and Donna

Contents

1

The Motivating Power
of the Cross

This book is a series of twelve messages on the Cross of the Lord Jesus Christ. Our Scripture is found in Titus 2:13-14:

> Looking for that blessed hope, and the glorious appearing of the great God and our Saviour Jesus Christ; Who gave himself for us, that he might redeem us from all iniquity, and purify unto himself a peculiar people, zealous of good works.

> For by grace are ye saved through faith; and that not of yourselves: it is the gift of God: Not of works, lest any man should boast. For we are his workmanship, created in Christ Jesus unto good works, which God hath before ordained that we should walk in them (Eph. 2:8-10).

Many people have told me with deep sadness that they never hear a message which relates to the Cross of Christ. But rather, the sermons are just on current events or social affairs. Let us now look at the scene on the Cross and all it might mean in every facet of our lives.

Look at the very motivating power of the Cross. Ephesians 2:8-9 is an often-quoted passage by Baptists because we love to talk about grace and faith. But when one comes to works, Baptists disagree. However, the Bible says in Ephesians 2:10 that not only are we saved by grace through faith, but that we are created in Christ Jesus unto good works—good works!

Then the passage from Titus is so essential, for it declares, "Looking for that blessed hope, and the glorious appearing of the great God and our Saviour Jesus Christ; Who gave himself for us, that he might redeem us from all iniquity, and purify unto himself a peculiar people."

We are saved that we might mature unto good works. That is the purpose of our having been born again, not only to go to heaven and to escape judgment but as Ephesians 2:8-10 says, so that we might produce good works. So, also, is the teaching of Titus 2:14, that we would be "zealous" toward good works.

Do you have a passion for Christian excellence? If I were to give this chapter another title, it would be: "The Desire for Christian Excellence," because God is saying that when a person is saved, the Cross is to make them "zealous," committed, excited about and enthusiastic for good works. How long has it been since you have been zealous to accomplish something great for God?

My first church members were all cotton farmers, and I saw all of the machinery, their laborers, their fertilizers, their insecticides, their equipment, and the land that was required. All of that involvement was for one simple product: a little boll of white fuzz called cotton. You might have asked those farmers, "Do you do all of this just for fun? Do you do it merely for exercise?"

"Oh no!"

"Why do you do it?"

They would respond, "We do it for one reason—that one day we might harvest a crop of those cotton bolls."

God did all He did, and Jesus came all the way for one

purpose—that you might one day produce fruit and be a fruit-bearing tree. I have noticed something about evergreen trees. Do you know where many evergreen trees are planted? In a cemetery! God doesn't want you to be a cedar. He doesn't want you to just look good. He wants you to be a fruit-bearing tree. I've never seen an orchard at a cemetery. After all, who would pick the fruit?

Too many church members are evergreens. They look good all the time but just don't produce anything, don't bear any fruit. All the work of the cotton farmer is toward the harvest. Likewise, all the work of redemption, all the plans of God, and all the sacrifice of Christ upon the Cross were in order that Titus 2:14 and Ephesians 2:10 might be fulfilled; that is, when we have been redeemed, we become "zealous unto good works!" Good works are the produce of our faith.

As I gaze at the Cross of Christ it is a motivation to me. And it ought to be a motivation to every believer when they know what Christ has done for them. He has redeemed you, and you have been born again by His wonderful blood. There is a marvelous motivating power in the Cross of Christ.

Let me share four factors that ought to motivate you regarding the Cross of Jesus Christ.

I. The Thundering of Thanksgiving

When lightning comes, thunder will follow. When lightning comes, there is an illumination of the sky, and there is the rolling and tumbling of thunder. So it is when lightning comes into your life, when you have the Light that illumines your life, then all of a sudden you begin to perceive what God has done for you.

All of a sudden you begin to have a vision of the Cross and a vision of His vicarious death, a vision of what it means that He was your substitute when He took your place on the Cross. When a lightning of revelation comes into your heart, there is welling up in you of gratitude, an expression of thanksgiving.

Now, the apostle Paul had much to be thankful for. He was educated at the feet of Gamaliel. Paul was a "Jew of the Jews," as he called himself. He was a man of wealth and of prominence. He had political connections. But this man of great accomplishments had decided not to know anything but Christ and Him crucified (1 Cor. 2:2). The apostle Paul, who was such an accomplished man, became a "one-subject man"—the Cross! Jesus and Him crucified! On the road to Damascus, when that shining light came literally out of the sky and blinded him, he became a changed man. That bolt of lightning started a thunderous roll of thanksgiving in his heart. All the days of his life, Paul lived for one purpose: that Jesus might be magnified in his life!

A. Thanksgiving Is Superior to Fear

Now fear is a strong motivation. In fact, the Bible says that people sinned because they feared not the face of God. So sometimes the fear of God keeps one from commiting wrong. Sometimes the fear of judgment helps one to come to know Christ as Savior. The Bible says, "The fear of the Lord is the beginning of wisdom" (Prov. 9:10).

I was reading where the president of the United States rides in a car that cost $500,000. That car has a jet canopy and three tons of reinforced steel. That car can take a bullet in the glass or in the metal up to .30 caliber without being penetrated. If one were to shoot out the tires of the president's car, he would see that even though the tires are flat, there is a metal disk inside every tire of the car carrying the president. Around that metal disk is a strip of hard rubber which is not inflated, so even if the tires were to blow out, the car could continue on for almost an indefinite time at 50 MPH.

What of all that care? Why all of those precautions? Fear! Officials fear that someone will do something silly or that someone will do something caustic and stupid and try to shoot the president of the United States. There is motivation in fear, but thanksgiving is far superior as a motivator.

B.   Thanksgiving Is Superior to Shame

Thanksgiving is not only superior to fear, it is also superior to shame. It is easy for us to grovel and confess, "Oh, it was my sins that put Him there. I'm so ashamed of how I've done." I could say, "Shame on you for not being present on Wednesday night! Shame on you for not giving like you should! Shame on you for not visiting! Shame on you for not loving God as you ought to! Shame on you!"

Don't do anything because you are ashamed. Love God because of what God has already done for you. Be motivated by thanksgiving. Sometimes when you try to shame another, you don't come up with the right conclusion anyway.

A butcher handed a little boy a package of meat scraps for his dog, and he had it wrapped in white butcher paper. He suggested, "Son, take these for your dog." The little boy walked away, but his mother grabbed him by the ear, dragged him over, and said, "Son, you didn't say anything to that butcher. What do you say?" He answered, "Charge it!" Shame is not always the right motivation.

C.   Thanksgiving Is Superior to Persuasion

To be thankful to God is superior to fear, superior to shame, but third: *it is superior to persuasion.* If I were to speak with the eloquence of an Apollos, with the pathos of an apostle Paul, with the rhetoric of a Demosthenes, and the oratory of a Cicero, then maybe someone listening to me would be persuaded to act. Maybe my power of eloquence, logic, and rationale could convince people they ought to be involved in the work of God. But persuade a man beyond his will, and he is of the same opinion still.

A grateful heart is a superior motive to fear, and it is a superior motive to intimidation or persuasion. You ought to teach a class, you ought to sing in the choir, you ought to read that Bible, you ought to pray, you ought to be out soul-winning, and you ought to give as you should because Jesus died for you. You still love Him. You still care for Him. You still love Him with all of your heart and soul!

Can you imagine in the early church some leader calling the Christians together and saying, "Look, you guys, not enough of you are showing up at the catacombs. I want you to give 10 percent of your income to the support of the catacombs. Where are you headed right now?"?

"Well, we're going to die in the Colosseum for Jesus."

"Oh, I see!"

Do you think any early Christian was persuaded to die in the Colosseum by some preacher? Do you think anyone went to the guillotine, put their heads down, and had their heads severed from their bodies because a preacher offered them a prize of a family Bible if they did? The motivation of all those in the New Testament and those in the early centuries who died horribly was that Jesus had died for them! How much can I do for Him?

My friend, we haven't started doing one iota for Jesus until we have given our life's blood for Him. That would be the only time you could come close to being for Him what He has been for you.

One of the motivating powers of my life is gratitude for the Cross. That's why Titus 2:14 says "zealous" unto good works.

II. The Temporary Triumph of Satan

Not only is the thundering of thanksgiving a factor in the motivating power of the Cross, there is also the temporary triumph of Satan.

When you and I gaze at the Cross, we view the grand economy and the great plan of God. Through the Cross humankind can be redeemed. Through the Cross mankind can be saved. But the devil thought that Calvary was his climactic hour. The devil knew the beginning of the Book of Genesis, where God declared to the serpent: "One day you will be able to bruise the heel of the One who will be the Messiah" (see Gen. 3:15). And Satan believed that on the Cross he had bruised the heel and that it was the Achilles Heel. He believed that he had put God out of business, that God was dead—like certain liberal theologians claimed a few years ago.

If there is one fact that motivates us to serve God and to love Him, it is this: the devil believed the Cross was his triumph. It was only temporary. For there suspended between heaven and earth was the Son of God, while down in hell there was a party and rejoicing. The demons must have celebrated in hell, chanting, "God is dead! God is dead! God is dead! We've done away with Jesus! No more power, no more miracles, no more healing, no more salvation, no more redemption, no more interference from heaven, and no more intervention from God because God is dead!"

It motivates me to take this Book and to preach it without compromise when I understand that the devil saw Calvary as a triumph, and I don't want him to have any more victories. I don't want to see Christ upon the Cross again. I have news for you—the Cross is empty!

We have a picture of Christ in our home, but He's not on the Cross. It's a picture of Christ smiling with His teeth showing. You don't see many pictures of Christ like that. I don't want to see Him dead and defeated by the devil. I want to see Him for what He is: risen and victorious! That motivates me to show the devil that it was not a victory for him; it was a victory for Christ!

After my father passed away, one of his relatives sent me a little package. I opened it up, and it was nothing but colored picture after colored picture of my Dad's casket, out at the cemetery, draped with sprays of lilies and flowers all around the casket. Below the casket one could see the hole in the ground where it was going to be lowered. My relative wrote that she knew I would enjoy these pictures and that I would like to have them. I kept those pictures less than thirty seconds! I didn't want to see those pictures of that casket, of those sprays of lilies, of those roses, of those potted plants, and that hole in the ground because Daddy wasn't there: he was with Jesus! He was kicking up dust on the streets of gold! He had walked through the gates of pearl!

I am going to so live, and I want you to so live, that the devil will never misunderstand. We don't serve a defeated and dead Lord: we serve a risen Savior! We're not going around despondent and discouraged with our heads down, thinking the world is coming to an end, that God is out business, and that God is dead. The devil is a loser!

In England right now there are 400 churches for sale. In England there is an office called "The Office of Church Demolition." They bulldoze churches down, so they can build a high-rise apartment or another type of building. I am talking about the fatherland of our faith. Why is America considered a Christian nation? Why has Christ been preached here for so long? It is because the people of England exported the faith and committed themselves to the Word of God in the colonies.

Many of the greatest preachers have been from London

like Charles Spurgeon. But the nation now has "gone to the devil." Only 7 percent of the people now attend any church. What happened to them? Ah, folks, the devil is winning victories! I have a word for you right now. I don't want to see a "For Sale" sign in front of First Southern Baptist Church or any church that upholds the Word. I wish with all of my heart—I pray that God right now would cause me to have a heart attack, and I'd die on this spot right this second rather than have that happen.

You reply, "Well, I'm just so discouraged. I'm just so down and out." There are many churches where you would fit in. Amen? Now we want one another to be together, to have unity, and to have power, and that is what we are going to do. Discouragement is one of the most effective tools of hell itself. We will not be discouraged. I will not be discouraged. You may comment, "Well, I'm going to tell you something that will discourage you . . ." You can't tell me anything that will discourage me. What if you predicted I'm going to die. I'd simply go to heaven encouraged. What motivates me to be more for God is the fact that the devil is waiting around like a vulture for one more temporary victory. We're going to kick the devil in the teeth, and we're going to shout, "God, You have the victory in us. Satan does not!"

III. The Mission Message of Calvary

Not only am I motivated by the thunderings of thanksgiving and the temporary triumph of Satan but also by the mission message of Calvary.

What is the mission message of Calvary? If you turn to Isaiah 53 or Psalm 22, you will note that even before the foundation of the earth Christ was the Crucified One. Even in prophecy, even as a little baby, He came to die. That was the message of Calvary. That motivates me.

18   NOTHING BUT THE BLOOD

There is a mission that could only be accomplished because of what He did on Calvary.

One artist has a picture of a brilliant Judean star as it shines through the latticework around the manger. As that star shines through the latticework, it has the picture of a shadowed cross upon the face of the baby Jesus while He lies in the manger. Even as an infant in Bethlehem's manger, upon that One the shadow of the Cross was focused.

Mohammed came to teach, Buddha came to demonstrate, Hinduism came for traditionalism, secular humanism has come to boost the egocentricity of man, but Jesus came as Savior! He came to save us from our sins, to redeem us. A message emanates from Calvary that could originate from no other place. Even His name Jesus is the Hebrew word *Joshua,* "He shall save his people" (Matt. 1:21). The name means, "For God so loved the world, that he gave his only begotten Son." Where did He give Him? He gave Him on Calvary. "That whosoever believeth in him should not perish" (John 3:16). What does perish mean? That they might not perish in an everlasting hell. Had Jesus merely wanted to teach, He would have lived to be ninety years old instead of thirty-three. He could have taught more in ninety years than He did in thirty-three, but He did not come primarily to teach. He came mainly to die. The message is that a person can be saved and saved unto good works if he or she will trust in Jesus as Lord and Savior.

What has made a difference in First Southern Baptist, Del City, down through the years? Do you know what has made a difference in Southern Baptist churches? It is because that we have known, through the years: when the invitation is given somebody, that some of you brought, was going to walk down the aisle. Somebody that you had won to Jesus would step out. What is different? When the invitation is given, people will be saved, people walk down the aisle, people will weep, and people will go to the altars. The day Southern Baptist churches quit having effective, God-honoring invitations is the when the churches will decline and be like any other mediocre church people can attend.

What has made some churches different is that they preach the gospel, they believe in the Holy Spirit, they believe that people can be saved, they believe that there is a hell to escape and a heaven to gain, the people have a warm heart for God, and they teach people how to win souls. That is the message of Calvary. Had Jesus simply wanted us to display principles, He would have lived to be ninety years old and taught and taught and taught. But He didn't come merely to teach: He came to die that people might be saved!

People have remarked to me across the country, "Preacher, what we want is to get fed." Normally, that's a sign of dreadful spiritual immaturity when these words come out of a person's lips. "We just want to get fed." What feeds me is seeing a person saved. I get "plum full" when a dear soul comes to Jesus. You may comment, "Preacher, we just want you to get up here and teach." God never called me to teach—God called me to preach. The difference in preaching and teaching is that, while there is always some teaching in good preaching, preaching always calls for a verdict for people to make a decision and for God to do a transformation. The world will never be changed by *information:* it is going to be changed by *inspiration* and *motivation.*

I left one church, and the pulpit committee decided, "We love Brother Bailey, but Brother Bailey's gift was evangelism, and he got all those people down the aisle, so what we're going to do now is to seek us out a teacher." They found a brilliant man to teach, and on the first Sunday morning he was there, he made the statement, "I don't care if we ever see another lost person in this church." He used an opaque projector and taught the people. Sunday School attendance dropped from 1,100 to 400.

People would call me weeping and moaning, "Oh, Brother Bailey, we no longer see the power of God in our services. We no longer feel conviction. We no longer see people transformed. We no longer see alcoholics becoming sober. We no longer see prostitutes being saved. We are no longer seeing homes brought back together. Our people are learning about spiritual gifts. They are learning about everything in the world, and the people are leaving the church like flies." My friend, the joy of God's heart is that a church honor what Jesus did upon the Cross, and what He did upon the Cross was to die that men and women might not have to die but that they might have everlasting life. That's the mission message of Calvary. Oh, God, give us glorious invitations that Your work might be honored. That motivates me! The mission message of the Cross is that people might be saved.

IV. The Cross Will Never Happen Again

Not only am I motivated by the thundering of thanksgiving and by the temporary triumph of Satan and by the mission message of Calvary, but also I'm motivated by the fact that the Cross will never happen again.

An ancient king in Prussia, when he would capture another king, would put him in prison, and every year he would bring the King out and humiliate him. They would stretch him out, and they would pull on him until he was a cripple. Then they would put the poor fellow back in prison, and the next year they would brutalize him again. Time and again, the imprisoned king would try to kill himself while he was in prison because he did not want to be brought out again and paraded around through enemy territory. My friend, Jesus died once for all.

It is written about Napoleon's men that they would follow him in snow, in ice, and subzero weather. They would die for him. When Napoleon walked onto the battlefield, it was equal to 500 new recruits because of the energy, enthusiasm, and invigoration of his very presence to the men in battle. His presence gave them a new zeal to fight; it gave them a new determination to win. Now, if men will do that for Napoleon who one day died, how much should you and I be motivated to sing in the choir, to teach that Sunday School class, and to be loyal to our church, because we serve a Lord who can never die?

Never again will there be a bogus court in front of Him. Never again will a disciple betray Him with a kiss. Never again will they scream, "Release unto us Barabbas and crucify Him." Never again will a Roman soldier put a spear into His side. Never again will a mocking soldier thrust vinegar and gall to His parched lips and make fun of His thirst, to make Him more thirsty—never again!

When He was here, He rode a donkey, but when He comes back, He will be on a white steed from heaven. When He was here, He loved His enemies, but when He comes back, His enemies will have to love Him. When He was here, He was sold for thirty pieces of silver, but when He comes back, He will be the Redeemer of the world. When He was here, He was buried in a borrowed tomb, but when He comes back, He will be reigning as King of kings and Lord of lords. When He was here, they put a crown of thorns upon His head, but when He comes back, He'll be wearing the diadem of Glory!

My friend, I am motivated by the fact that the Lord I serve will never, never die again. "He ever liveth making intercession for us." The Cross of Christ motivates me.

They asked the mighty man of God, Count Zinzendorf,

how he stayed so faithful to Christ. He replied, "On yonder wall." Then he pointed to a picture of the Cross, the Cross on Calvary. Underneath the picture of the Cross were these words, "All this for thee, how much for Me? All this for thee, how much for Me?" Count Zinzendorf testified that every day when he looked at that picture, he thought, *The Lord is speaking to me: "All this for thee, how much for Me"?*

Steinberg used to bring a little Gypsy girl into his art studio, and she would sit for him on occasion. When he was painting his famous picture of Christ upon the Cross, she asked him one day, "Is that a mean man? Is that why they killed Him like that and put Him upon that Cross?" Steinberg protested, "Oh, no! He was a very good man. In fact some people think He was the best man who ever lived. But you see, He was dying for others." The Gypsy girl, not intending to, became a marvelous witness as she asked, "Well, Mr. Steinberg, did He die for you?" My friend, the question today is: "Did He die for you? Did He die for you?"

I want you to see Jesus—see that Cross and remember those words that changed Count Zinzendorf's life: "I did all this for thee, how much for Me?" The motivating power of the Cross!

2

Offended by the Opportunity to Live

A little leaven leaveneth the whole lump. I have confidence in you through the Lord, that ye will be none otherwise minded: but he that troubleth you shall bear his judgment, whosoever he be (Gal. 5:9-11).

A little boy ran into his mother's arms and yelled, "Mama, I just saw a big gorilla in our front yard." She chided, "Son, you go up to your bedroom and ask God to forgive you for that. You know there isn't a gorilla in our front yard." (It really was the big Saint Bernard dog from across the street.)

About ten minutes later the boy came down from his bedroom, and the mother asked, "Son, did you ask God to forgive you?" "Yes, Ma'am, I did." "Well, what did God say?" He said, "Well, Son, don't worry about it. The first time I saw that dog, I thought it was a gorilla too!" Now, you can't always go by appearances. Human beings have often gotten into trouble with appearances. If one were to judge the Cross by appearances, one would always judge it offensively.

Galatians 5:9-11 contains one of the real mysteries of

the Bible. Paul was explaining to the churches of Galatia that they were at a very critical moment of their testimony. Many people were telling them that they had to add something to their faith, and that the gospel was not enough. The Greek word *kervgma*, the full gospel, was not enough. So they had to add something to it, and of course the doctrine of that day was to add circumcision to faith in Christ.

Paul wrote, "I know that if I were to teach you that, then the Cross would not be an offense to you any longer" Paul would not compromise the truth. The fact is that we don't need anything, not even circumcision, added to the salvation message (see v. 6). It is the Cross, it is the Blood, it is what Jesus did, and that is adequate. That's enough!

Still, Paul was pointing out an essential truth. That is, to the modern mind the Cross of Christ (Gal. 5:11) is an offensive message. That is why I have entitled this chapter "Offended by the Opportunity to Live." Why would people be offended by that very thing which promises them life?

You and I have heard the stories of drowning people who have fought off lifeguards as the lifeguards were trying to save their lives. In their panic, the victims did not know what they were doing. Yet all around you every day, there are untold millions of people who are literally fighting off the truth of salvation. They are doing all they can to die and to avoid life. They are offended by the opportunity to live!

Do you know why people are offended? People are offended because, just as in my illustration at the beginning, they see only what appears to be, not what really is. Why are people offended by the gospel of the Cross of Christ? There is an offense to the preaching of the gospel. Let me suggest four reasons why people are offended by the preaching of the Cross.

I. The Cross Appears to Be Defeat

They are offended by the Cross because the Cross appears to be defeat. It is actually victory! People of that day did not want a loser; neither do people of today. When they saw the Cross, they thought of Jesus Christ as a loser —someone who had gotten himself into deep trouble by being arrested. It a strange quirk about human nature that we like a winner, even when the winner is not worthy of being liked.

When people were being interviewed in a certain state as to why they were going to vote for a certain candidate in the gubernatorial race, they answered, "We know he's a womanizer, and we know he loves to gamble and to get drunk, but we're going to elect him anyway!" I read recently where the man is being indicted for a serious crime.

It is interesting that there is a quality in the human psyche which says, "I like a man that's confident and arrogant whether or not he is morally correct." Do you remember when the choice was given to the crowd that day in Pilate's hall? Whom shall we release? And they said, "Barabbas" (Matt. 27:21). Ah, but he was a common criminal. He was a revolutionary. He was a rebel.

They thought to themselves, *We would rather have Barabbas in the streets raping our daughters, than Jesus Christ saving them.* When Jesus stood before Pilate, He didn't pop off. In fact the Bible says, "He answered nothing" (Matt. 27:12). *We don't want this weak, emaciated Nazarene. What we want is Barabbas! A he-man! The playboy philosophy! Man, we like Barabbas-type fellows. That is what we like!*

The world is still like that. They saw Barabbas as a winner, but Jesus as nothing but a weak loser. They saw defeat. No wonder Paul wrote in 1 Corinthians that the

Cross was a stumblingblock to the Jews (1:23). Why shouldn't it be a stumblingblock to the Jews, because all the Jews had ever known was defeat and trouble? They were defeated by the Assyrians, by the Babylonians, by the Romans, by the Greeks? They had been captives to the Egyptians. Jerusalem was always in a period of war. Soldiers were always sieging Jerusalem.

Even at the very beginning of Jesus' earthly life, Rome loomed over the city of Jerusalem like a fearsome shadow. So of all people to support a loser, it would not be the Jewish people who had known one tragedy, one heartache, one bondage, and one period of persecution after another. They saw one word: defeat . . . defeat . . . defeat!

While the Cross may be an offense to people because they view it as a defeat, the Bible declares that the Cross was not a defeat but a victory! Here are five areas where the Cross was a victorious event:

A. Jesus Was Not Diverted from His Purpose

The Cross was victorious because Jesus was not diverted from His purpose. Had Jesus not died on the Cross, He would have been out of the will of God. Had Jesus not died on the Cross, He would not have fulfilled God's purpose in His coming for people to trust Jesus Christ as Lord and Savior. While other religions have similar teachings to Christianity, no one has a Savior!

Buddhism teaches many principles akin to Christianity. Mohammed copied many of Jesus' teachings. When we come to the works of Shintoism or Zoroastrianism, we discover some parallels to the Christian faith. But there is something no other religion has, and that is a Savior. No other religion has One who died on a Cross or anywhere else in a propitiating manner, in a vicarious way, for those who would follow Him.

You see, the world does not need a guru because the

problem is not religion. The world does not need a teacher because the problem is not ignorance. The world does not need a nationalist because the problem is not politics; but the world does need a Savior because the problem is sin! It was Jesus who died upon that Cross, and had He not died, His very purpose in coming to be our Savior would have been diverted.

B. Jesus Fulfilled the Sacrificial System

The Cross was victorious because it was the fulfillment of the sacrificial system. In the days of the Levitical priesthood, the priest on the Day of Atonement would bring a lamb to the Temple. On the brazen altar he would sacrifice that lamb. The lamb would pay the ultimate price for sin, which is death. Then the high priest would enter the Holy of Holies with the shed blood of the lamb.

Remember that the blood of bulls and goats and lambs had no real power to forgive people of their sins. It only forgave men of their sins to this extent: that God promised if they were to do that, He would honor their obedience to Him by forgiving their sins. Had Jesus Christ Himself, being the Lamb of God that takes away the sin of the world, not died, then all of the Old Testament typology would have fallen. But Jesus fulfilled His purpose as the Paschal Lamb, the sacrificial Lamb, in dying upon that Cross and shedding His blood for the world.

Remember that when Jesus began His ministry, Satan found Him in the wilderness and tempted Him sorely. Jesus was hungry, and Satan inquired, "Why Jesus, you are all powerful, why don't You take these stones and turn them to bread?"

Then Satan told Him, "Jesus, throw yourself down from this pinnacle." The reason Satan wanted Jesus to die then was because he knew that if Jesus made it all the way to the Cross and died, fulfilling the sacrificial system, then

Satan would be washed up. Satan would be through because there is one act he cannot do: he cannot make anyone lost and bound for hell who has already been washed in the blood.

C. Jesus Died a Kingly Death

A third area where the Cross was victorious is the fact that Jesus died a kingly death. As the women were weeping over Jesus, He said, "Weep not for me, but weep for yourselves, and for your children" (Luke 23:28). A Roman soldier rudely tried to throw Him to the Cross, and Jesus asserted, "No man takes my life from me, I lay it down freely for my brethren" (see John 10:18).

Compare that to Job who said, "I know that my redeemer liveth, [and] in my flesh shall I see God: Whom I shall see for myself, and mine eyes shall behold, and not another" (Job 19:25-27).

I think of Voltaire the atheist who chortled that he would put Christianity out of business. But on his deathbed, Voltaire cried, "Even though I have not taken my last breath, I feel the flames of hell! I am a wretched man!"

My friend, one dies the way one lives. Jesus died a kingly death because He was the King of kings and Lord of lords.

D. Jesus Died Willingly

There is a fourth reason why I know the Cross was a victorious event. It is the fact that Jesus died willingly! That was His great purpose, His great goal, His great intention.

Some at the crucifixion shouted, "He saved others; himself he cannot save" (Matt. 27:42). My friend, it was not those nails in His hands that held Him to the Cross, and it was not those nails in His feet which pinioned Him there. It was the golden cords of love that strapped Him to that Roman Cross as He died for you and me.

E. Jesus Died a Complete Death.

Here is a fifth reason that the Cross was a victory. It was victorious because Jesus died a complete death. Jesus on that Cross screamed out those words, translated into the Greek, *"Tetelestai!" "It is finished"* (John 19:30).

Jesus did not cry "I am finished" because He was not finished, but *it* was finished. You ask, "What was finished?" All He had to do to accomplish our redemption, our salvation was finished. Heaven's gates were opened to all who would receive Him.

I was in the Methodist Hospital at Dallas, Texas, one time, and down the hall came a loud, raucous group of people. I heard one man using profanity. When they passed me, I stepped out to see what was going on down the hall, and they were giving a doctor a hard time. What had happened was this: the family had brought in their mom for surgery. She had an infected eye and could see out of only one eye. The doctor had taken out the good eye and had left her totally blind.

The family, as you can imagine, was distraught, frustrated, and angry at such a moment. I thought how *I* could make a mistake, how a physician could make a mistake, or how an attorney could make a mistake.

When Jesus Christ went to the Cross, everything needed for our salvation was done, exactly as it should have been done. He did it right; he did it properly. He made no mistakes. There were no errors. All was done in keeping with the prophetic truth of the Old Testament that your salvation might be bought and paid for. Yes, the Cross is an offense to people because it appears to be defeat, but in reality it is victory.

II. The Cross Appears to Be the Wrong Way

There is a second thought about the preaching of the Cross. It is an offense to people because it appears to be the wrong way but indeed is the right way. Now, you see, humanity never would have thought up the idea of sacrificing someone to allow someone else to be alive. Humans would never have come up with that idea; humans always get things backwards. Nothing is more offensive to people than for God to have His own way.

In fact, the word Paul uses in Galatians 5:11 for "offence" is the Greek word *skandalon*. It is the word from which we receive our words *scandal* or *scandalous*. People think the Cross is scandalous, that it is a scandal that Jesus would have to die on the Cross.

Why do you think that would be so? Well, if you go back and study the Book of Galatians, you will understand why the Cross is scandalous. The Judaizers were teaching that, yes, one needed to trust Christ, but even that was not good enough unless one were also circumcised. It was nothing but a carry-over from their Judaistic backgrounds.

They claimed that if one were to bring in that doctrine plus Jesus, then one would be all right. Jesus alone was not enough for them. After all, the Jewish teachers were teaching that there must be a circumcision, the symbol of doing away with the old flesh and the coming of the new law. Paul said, "Oh, yes, if I were to agree with you, then there would not be an 'offence' to my gospel." "But," he countered, "You are offended when I tell you that you don't need anything except what Jesus did on the Cross. You might be offended, but I'm not going to change my mind because what I have told you is exactly the truth" (based on Gal. 5).

The Jewish teachers replied, "Law." The Sadducees

contended, "Intellectualism." The Pharisees emphasized, "Ceremony." The Greeks cried, "Culture." The Epicureans chortled, "Pleasure and fun—that's where it is!" The Athenian scholars boasted, "Science." But God declared "The Cross!"

Jesus came to do away with artificial religion that people might know salvation. But that is offensive. It is an offense because it does away with one's own religion. It does away with denominational distinctions. It does away with man-made religious "hype." It does away with certain gimmicks some preachers have made a living on. It literally chisels away all the artificial stuff and comes down to the basic ingredient, and that is: "without the shedding of blood there is no remission of sin." You cannot add one iota to it!

Mormonism has tried to add the writings of a man, Joseph Smith, and his Book of Mormon. To believe that is to avoid the truth and to avoid salvation. Jehovah's Witnesses have tried to add all of their materials and to lead men away from the central focus of the Cross.

One time my wife and I visited a church that had on one side of the altar a little pulpit behind which a man stood. On the other side was another pulpit behind which a lady stood. There was a Bible on one pulpit. The works of Mary Baker Eddy were on the other pulpit. The lady read the doctrines of Christian Science, and the man would read a Scripture. There was one pulpit and one book too many! Christian Science is neither Christian nor science.

You reply, "Brother Bailey, you shouldn't talk that way about other religions." Listen, you don't even need to be a Baptist to get to heaven!

One of the biggest religions I know in the world is that of Baptists! Many folks had Baptist "religion" before they had Jesus. Amen? Many people had a local church before they had Jesus. That is why the Cross is offensive to people who are not spiritually sensitive to the work of the Holy Spirit in their lives.

They are offended when somebody stands up and preaches like the apostle Paul did to the Galatians: No, you don't need the old law. No, you don't need circumcision. No, you don't need all that ritualism. All you need to know is: once you were a sinner; Jesus died on the Cross for your sin; He paid the price for your iniquity. He is your Redeemer, and when He died upon that Cross, He did away with the guilt of all your sins.

You are now at liberty. Quit putting yourself back into the bonds of the old law and the old system. You have been set free by the Cross of Christ.

Why should people be offended by the opportunity to live? Only because deep down in human hearts, people are full of personal ego, and they cannot imagine God doing something for them that they cannot do for themselves. But that is one trip you cannot make for yourself. God has to make it for you. "Jesus paid it all,/All to him I owe;/Sin had left a crimson stain,/He wash'd it white as snow."

I was talking with Elvis Presley's stepbrother, Rick Stanley, sometime ago, and I said, "Rick, you are not before an audience right now. How about Elvis and his relationship to Christ? I know he watched Rex Humbard who preached his funeral. I don't know anybody better than Rex Humbard. He is a good, genuine man."

He answered, "That's right, Bailey, but Elvis's problem was that in the last years of his life, the only thing he did was read the books of Eastern cults and religions." I asked, "Why?" Rick answered, "Well, Elvis and I were sitting on the bed one night, and I asked him why he was reading a certain book, and he said to me, 'Well, Rick, I have been with a lot of outstanding people lately, and they tell me that the gospel could not be true because it is too simple. I want something else!' "

Folks, you don't need a weird-looking guru to get you to heaven. You don't need an Eastern cult. You don't even need Bailey Smith! All you need to do is know that you are a worthless, hell-bound sinner, Jesus died for you, and if you commit your life to Him and what He did upon the Cross, you are on the road to heaven.

In my weak moments I would like to tell you that you have to be a member of the church. I would like to say that you have to be a Southern Baptist. But I have to tell you the truth, and the truth of the matter is: without the shedding of blood there is no forgiveness of sin. When you come via the Cross, that is the way home, and nothing that human beings can add to this will draw you any closer at all to heaven. The only way you can be saved is through what Jesus did on that Cross!

Some may ask, "Bailey, do you think there might be room for another way?" No way! That cannot be! "How are you so sure?" I'll tell you why I am so sure. People say you love God, and He is a God of love. They belong to a group like Unity which teaches great ethics or Bahai which adds a little of the ethical teachings from four or five different religions. They say that is what they want—just a God of love—not a God that singles out Jesus and the avenue of the Cross. Is that what you want? You cannot have it!

Let me explain why. If there were some other way to get to heaven besides Jesus, the Son of God, dying on the Cross, and God went ahead with allowing the murder of His boy when there was another way, God would be too mean and cruel for you to worship. God would be too mean and cruel for you even to adore. He would not be a God of love; He would not be a God of ethics; He would not be a God of high standards.

I remember when our son Stephen was just a little bitty fellow, he had a raging fever all night long. It went up to 104°; we called the doctor and asked, "What shall we do?" The doctor replied, "What you have to do is fill your bathtub with ice-cold water. Don't put any of the warm water in at all. Then take off his clothes and put him up to his chin in that cold water."

Sandy looked at me and said, "When are you going to do it?" I went in, and Stephen was, of course, warm in his bed. He had on pajamas with feet in them. I carried Stephen in, and I had already filled that tub with ice-cold water. I took off those little pajamas, and I put him in quickly, submerged in that water up to his chin. I have never seen such a horrified look on anyone's face in my life.

He looked up at me and remarked, "Daddy, you're a dodo bird. How could you do this to me? How could you treat me this way?"

If there had been an easier way for me to bring that fever down, I wouldn't have treated my little son like that. I was doing what I believed to be right. Had God known any other way to save us, other than somebody paying the price for our ugly sin in the form of Jesus, He would have done it. Do you think He wanted His Son to go to the Cross? Absolutely not! Do you think Jesus eagerly ran up and jumped on that Cross and had a high old time? No!

He fulfilled the biblical truth that blood had to be shed; a sacrifice had to be made. Someone had to pay the price for our sins. Either Jesus paid it on the Cross, or we will pay it in hell. Those are the only choices. Jesus paid the ultimate sacrifice.

III. The Cross Appears to Be Death

The third reason people are offended by the preaching of the Cross is: first of all, the Cross *appears* to be defeat but is victory; it *appears* to be the wrong way for salvation but is the right way; and the Cross appears to be death but is really life. The crowds looked at that Cross and that blood, and they saw the brutality—the bleeding and the torn flesh. They viewed the horrible sight of that gruesome experience of Christ.

They could smell the stench of death, and they said, "Death, we don't want you." Even Jesus said, in essence, "When you pick up the Cross and follow me, that means you must die" If we translate that Scripture correctly, it means that if we want to follow Christ, then we have to pick up our electric chair and follow Him.

The Cross was a picture of execution, and when people looked at the Cross, they cried, "Death is offensive." That is why the "think-positive" churches are so popular today. They want little tidbits of positive-thinking sermonettes, not the deep truths of the Cross.

Some think, *Give us something shallow on the surface so we may go out and make more money in our businesses, but don't teach us the offensive doctrine of the Cross. That is ugly, that is gruesome, and that is deathful.*

Many love the Cross as a trinket: a Cross on a colonial, red-brick church with white pillars, a white cross on top of the steeple. That is fine but not the real Cross! Not the Cross of the hill of the skull, not the Cross of Golgotha, not the Cross of Calvary—give us something else, but not that Cross.

I saw a tennis player who was using ugly words and, in a clandestine way, was making obscene gestures to the referee. The player had a gold cross on a chain around his neck while he was using profanity and making crude gestures. I thought to myself, *He has no right to wear that cross.*

My friend, you have no right to wear a Cross unless you have been born again and unless your sins have been

forgiven by what happened on that Cross, it is blasphe-
mous. You will face the judgment of God if you display a
Cross on your body, and you have not experienced what
Jesus Christ did upon that Cross. You see, people look at
that and think, *Death: we don't want that. Death is so
horrible.*

Years ago in Tucson, Arizona, I was conducting a revival, and the pastor asked me to talk with a wealthy man
who had never given his life to Christ. He had recently
bought a new Jaguar, for which he had paid $35,000. They
cost far more now. As we were driving around the city of
Tucson, I noticed a beautiful piece of ground at a cemetery. Flowers were everywhere. There were beautiful
eucalyptus trees.

I commented, off the top of my head, "Isn't that a
beautiful cemetery?" He shivered, "Ugh, I have never
seen a beautiful cemetery." I replied, "Well, I mean the
flowers are blooming, and those eucalyptus trees are so
pretty." For about forty-five seconds he was silent. Then
he mused, "You know, I would like to live—someday—
where there is no cemetery." You talk about an opening
for a witness! I immediately answered, "I can tell you
about a country where there is no cemetery." And there
is no death there!

When people looked at the Cross, it became offensive
to them because they thought it was death. But it was life.

Fanny Crosby wrote over 500 gospel songs. As you
know, she was blind all of her life because a country doctor accidentally spilled acid in her eyes when she was a
baby. Dwight L. Moody one time explained to Fanny
Crosby, "Fanny, I want you to know I have been praying
that one day God will heal you and give you eyesight."

Her reply: "Moody, I've been praying God would never
heal me."

"But, Fanny, I thought before you die, you would like to see something."

"Oh, no. God's never going to heal me. Don't ever ask for God to heal me."

"But, Fanny, wouldn't you like to see?" She said, "No, just imagine it! If I do not get healing, the first sight I will ever see will be the face of Jesus." That is a beautiful testimony.

Fanny Crosby heard, in Chicago, of a man claiming to be a messiah, and she despised the fact that a man would claim to take the place of Jesus. Miss Crosby decided to write a song and dedicate it to the work of the Salvation Army. She met with the Salvation Army band one day when she heard that the "messiah" and his followers were going to come walking down a street in Chicago. She decided to stand on the street with those Salvation Army people, and they were going to sing her new song.

Down one side of that street came that false prophet, who claimed to be Jesus, with a host of people. Down the other side came the Salvation Army band playing Fanny Crosby's new song. Do you know what the song was? "I shall know Him, I shall know Him, by the prints of the nails in His hands. I shall know Him, I shall know Him, by the prints of the nails in His hands."

As the Salvation Army band and the singers came even with that self-proclaimed messiah with his hundred followers, one of those following the fake messiah all of a sudden went in front of that man, grabbed his hands, and looked at them. He yelled, "You have no scars! We hear the Salvation Army singing that we shall know Him by the prints of the nails in His hands. You have no nail prints! You are a fake!"

All of a sudden, those one hundred people—instead of following that messiah—turned their direction and started marching with the Salvation Army band, and they were all singing, "I shall know Him by the prints of the nails in His hands."

My friend, that is how we will know Him! Do you know that all of us when we get to heaven will have no more scars? When I reach heaven I am going to have a lot of blond, bushy hair! Those of you who are crippled will not need your crutches. Those of you who are blind will be able to see. Those of you who are deaf will need no one to interpret with their hands.

But there is One who will not be rid of His scars. Jesus will be scarred throughout all of eternity as a reminder to you and me that it was the Cross that got us to heaven. It appeared to be death, but it was life.

IV. The Cross Appears to Be the End

People are also offended by the preaching of the Cross because the Cross appears to be the end, but it is only the beginning.

The disciples were discouraged, the friends were frightened, their fondest dreams were turned to nightmares, and they lamented, "It's over, it's over, it's over! What are we going to do?" The Cross is not the end. It is only the beginning.

Now it appears to be the end, but that is the limited wisdom of human beings. Let me suggest four things that it began.

A. The Cross Began a New Mission

Never before had people been able to declare, "Jesus has died on the cross." After the Cross Jesus gave the Great Commission and told His followers to go out, win, teach, and baptize in the name of the Father and of the Son and of the Holy Ghost. You and I know that Jesus has died, and our sins have been atoned for because Jesus Christ is the Redeemer.

We have a new mission, and it is an empowered one. The mission God has given us is to be soul-winners and to spread the news that Jesus died once and for all: "Though your sins be as scarlet, they shall be as white as snow" (Isa. 1:18). We have a new mission.

B. The Cross Began a New Manifestation

In the Old Testament, God was manifested as God the Father. He wrote the tables of stone for Moses. He gave a pillar of fire and a pillar of cloud for the Israelites to follow. He also rolled back the Red Sea so the children of Israel could escape the Egyptians.

In the New Testament dispensation, we have God the Son, the Lord Jesus Christ, whose footprints were in the sands of Galilee's shore. That was the New Testament manifestation.

What do we have today? We do not have God the Father doing such acts as He did in the Old Testament days. We do not have God the Son in the flesh walking around our neighborhoods, our shopping centers, and our marketplaces. We have God the Holy Spirit.

Some may ask, "Brother Bailey, wouldn't it be great to live in the Old Testament? Wouldn't it be wonderful to live in the New Testament?" God has never been more present on earth than He is today. The manifestation of the Holy Spirit is just as real as the manifestation of God the Son and God the Father. It is just as real! It is a new, living manifestation.

What did Jesus mean when He said in John 14:12 that He was going to leave, and that He was going to leave a new manifestation of Himself, the Person of the Holy Ghost? He said, "When I leave and when I send you the Holy Ghost, you will be able to do greater things than I have done" (see John 14:12). Now that is hard for me to believe, that I can do greater things than Jesus. What He meant was this: even when He was upon this earth, He could only be at one place at one time, but when He left, the Holy Ghost would be in the people gathered on Pentecost and in those born-again Christians living today.

Jesus taught that when He went to the Father, He would "leave Myself in a broader way upon this earth." That is because the Holy Spirit is in that born-again black man in Africa, in that saved red man somewhere on this earth, in that redeemed yellow man, in that Christian white man, in that blood-bought brown man, in that delivered illiterate man, in that saved educated man, in that ransomed intellectual man, in that Christian rich man, and in that believing poor man. Christ is here more than He has ever been, through the agency of the Holy Spirit. "You will be able to do greater things than I have done," indicated Jesus.

C.   The Cross Began a New Ministry

The Cross not only began a new mission of soul-winning, and not only a new manifestation of the Holy Spirit, but the Cross also began a new ministry.

Do you know what never existed before the Cross? Spiritual gifts. Do you know that when Jesus Christ died on the Cross and the Holy Spirit came so vibrantly, that was the beginning of spiritual gifts.

Some of you exercise your spiritual gifts when you teach a Sunday School class. Some of you do it when you minister by getting the coffee cups and the doughnuts. Some of you have the gift of administration. We can name fourteen or nineteen spiritual gifts, depending on how we count them.

But all those spiritual gifts became a reality after the death of Jesus upon the Cross. The Cross was not the end. It was the beginning of a new mission, a new manifestation, and a new ministry.

D. The Cross Began a New Might

The Cross was also the beginning of a new might. In Acts 1:8, Jesus said, "But ye shall receive power, after that the Holy Ghost is come upon you."

The Greek word for power is *dunamis*, from which we derive the word *dynamite*. Jesus said, "After I leave, you are going to receive a power that has never before been available."

So the Cross was not the end, it was the beginning. You and I have a *dunamis*, we have a power to shake this world like we cannot imagine. *Dunamis!* You shall receive power when the Holy Spirit has come upon you.

Several years ago in San Diego, a ship strayed off course and became stuck on a reef at low tide. Twelve tugboats were brought, and they put hawsers from the tugs to the ship and tried to pull it, but that did not work.

Then the tugs moved to one side and tried to push the ship off of the reef. Black smoke was belching everywhere. The water around the big vessel had turned to a white foam with the twelve tugs pushing with all their mighty power against that ship. They could not budge it!

Finally, the captain instructed the little tugs to go back home. He sighed, "I'll just be patient and wait." He waited until high tide. All of a sudden the ocean began to rise, and what human power could not do, the rising tide of the Pacific Ocean did by lifting that ship and putting it back into the channel.

I am grateful for what organization and promotion can do, but what our churches need to do is to wait upon the irresistible power of the Holy Spirit. We need to wait until God lifts us into a channel that we could never have known apart from His tremendous power. We have a new mission; we have a new manifestation; we have a new ministry of spiritual gifts, and we have a new might. In Jesus' name we have a new power that can never fail.

I beg of you—do not be offended by the opportunity to live!

3

The Problems of Pilate

When he was set down on the judgment seat, his wife sent unto him, saying, Have thou nothing to do with that just man: for I have suffered many things this day in a dream because of him. But the chief priests and elders persuaded the multitude that they should ask Barabbas, and destroy Jesus. The governor answered and said unto them, Whether of the twain will ye that I release unto you? They said, Barabbas. Pilate saith unto them, What shall I do then with Jesus which is called Christ? They all say unto him, Let him be crucified. And the governor said, Why, what evil hath he done? But they cried out the more, saying, Let him be crucified. When Pilate saw that he could prevail nothing, but that rather a tumult was made, he took water, and washed his hands before the multitude, saying, I am innocent of the blood of this just person: see ye to it. Then answered all the people, and said, His blood be on us, and on our children (Matt. 27:19-25).

I remember years ago listening to Dr. Herschel H. Hobbs preach on "The Baptist Hour" about Pontius Pilate. He stated that Pilate tried to do everything he could to avoid contact with Jesus.

Dr. Hobbs, in his inimitable manner, described that scene as Pilate stood before Jesus, and Jesus stood before

Pilate. He began to describe the various words and actions Pilate tried to do in his encounter with Christ.

Hobbs preached, first of all, that Pilate tried to ignore the fact that Jesus was there. He tried to say, "This man has done nothing really bad; let's go on to something else." He tried to look in another place. He even spoke to the crowd about the holiday. Pilate tried to do all he could to ignore the presence of Jesus. That did not work because the crowd would not let it.

Pilate then tried admiration. He testified about Jesus, "I find no fault in this man." He thought that if he could simply admire Jesus, then that would be enough. We have people like that today who admire Jesus in literature, in art, in culture. Yet they have never met Jesus personally.

Since ignoring Jesus did not do it, and admiring Jesus did not do it, Dr. Hobbs observed that Pilate tried to shift the responsibility.

In Luke 23, we discover that Pilate sent Jesus to Herod, since Herod was in town for the Passover. Herod, of course, later sent Jesus back to Pilate. Anytime we try to send Jesus away, He always comes back. We always have to stand before Jesus. We always have to encounter Him. Shifting the responsibility did not work either.

Finally, Dr. Hobbs preached that Pilate tried substitution. He tried to be kind to somebody else: Barabbas. He released and set him free. When you face Christ and the need of salvation, there is no substitute for Jesus Christ. You cannot go to Mohammed, to Eastern religions, to positive thinking, or to religious idealism. You cannot go anywhere else to find what is exclusively and uniquely available in Jesus Christ!

Dr. Hobbs closed his brilliant message with the idea that Pilate began to diminish his guilt by claiming the death of Christ was another's responsibility. Hobbs described how Pilate blamed the multitude for the demise of this man of Nazareth, Jesus Christ.

We are going to examine the problems that Pilate had, problems which many people face inevitably today.

I. Problem One—Pilate Faced Popularity Without Principle

Pilate faced popularity without principle. If there is one truth we learn from reading Luke's, Mark's, and Matthew's accounts of this incident, it is that, above all else, Pilate wanted to be popular. The Bible indicates that out of fear Pilate did what the crowd wanted. He could not control the multitude. Pilate feared that a riot would break loose, so he decided to do what the crowd suggested.

As I look at this passage, I do not notice that Pilate was an aggressive militant. I do not find him doing evil to Christ. In fact, I truly believe down deep in my heart that the governor believed Jesus was a good guy; Jesus was all right, and he had done nothing worthy of death.

Pilate was like many today who believe in God as long as it does not cost them. They will "follow Christ" until it begins to cost. Pilate was willing to serve the good of Jesus as long as he did not have to pay a price for it.

The multitude screamed, "Crucify Him! Crucify Him!" (see Matt. 23:21). They yelled, "If you let Jesus go, you're no friend of Caesar" (paraphrase of John 19:12). "But, this is your king," Pilate protested to the Jews. The Jews answered, "We have no king but Caesar" (John 19:15). Pilate was caught between doing what was right and what was popular. Have you ever been there? I have. Have you ever been caught smack between those two dreadfully hard positions of deciding between the right thing to do and the acceptable thing to do?—that is, acceptable by your peers, acceptable by your friends, or acceptable by your society.

Pontius Pilate was there. He knew that Jesus should not be condemned. On the other hand, the governor knew the crowd wanted Him to be condemned.

So, what does a man do? He does according to what he is made of. In Pilate's case, it was soft, mushy, and pliable. He followed expediency. He did whatever feathered his own cap. He did whatever filled his moneybags, whatever added to his own political camp.

Pilate made the most expedient choice he could: "I'll tell you what you do. You just do whatever you want to. I want to be accepted by you. I want to be popular."

Grant Teaff, the head football coach of Baylor University, was our guest speaker at First Southern Baptist, Del City. As we were seated at the table looking at the more than five hundred men present, Coach Teaff leaned over and asked, "What do these men expect?" I answered, "They expect for you to say whatever you want to say."

He commented, "Well, here we are at a Holiday Inn. We are not exactly at church. Bailey, I think it would be a mistake for me to come this far and not tell these men the greatest news I know." "Coach, have at it!" I exulted.

"Do you care if I give an invitation?" Teaff inquired. Now, can you believe it, a coach asking a preacher: "Do you care if I give an invitation?" "Go ahead and give an invitation, " I urged. From the beginning of the first sentence until he closed out, Coach Teaff preached Jesus. He talked about the call of God upon his life and upon his family, how God had led him in his marriage and in bringing up his daughters. In every area of his life the coach preached Christ. Why? He did that out of his heart. He did not decide to be popular; he decided to share what was on his heart. That is what a Christian person is called to do.

A friend of mine mentioned that he was asked by the Chamber of Commerce, in the Tennessee city where he lives, "to say the invocation." I am always a little suspicious when I am asked to "say" an invocation. I always want to jump up and say, "Invocation. Amen!" He answered, "I will be glad to say your invocation at the Chamber of Commerce meeting."

The day before he was to "say the invocation" at that meeting, an attorney called, saying, "Pastor, we appreciate your agreeing to come to pray, but I need to ask you something."

"Sure, anything." The attorney asked, "When you come to pray, you don't plan to pray in Jesus' name, do you?"

"Yes, sir, I normally do." The attorney inquired, "Don't you have a nonsectarian prayer?"

"Well, I really do not have a prayer like that."

Folks, you do not "say" prayers. You talk to God. If you do not talk through Jesus' name, you do not talk to God! What that pastor said is exactly my sentiment. He said, "I really appreciate the honor of getting to say your invocation, but if you don't mind, find yourself a nonsectarian preacher!" Find somebody that doesn't stand for anything, somebody that accepts prayer as ecclesiastical verbiage for itching ears.

When people pray, they ought to talk to God, and they ought to go to the throne in Jesus' name. They ought to have the bathing of the Holy Spirit.

Let us do a little Bible Study on courage. In Acts 4, we see men who decided to be men of principle and not men of popularity.

> They called them, and commanded them not to speak at all nor teach in the name of Jesus. But Peter and John answered and said unto them, Whether it be right in the sight of God to hearken unto you more than unto God, judge ye. For we cannot but speak the things which we have seen and heard. (vv. 18-20).

> Acts 5:28-29:—Did not we straitly command you that ye
> should not teach in this name? and, behold, ye have filled Jerusa-
> lem with your doctrine, and intend to bring this man's blood
> upon us. Then Peter and the other apostles answered and said,
> We ought to obey God rather than men.

Amen for that. Here were men of principle instead of
men of popularity. In Acts 21, we discover that the apostle
Paul was told by God to go to Jerusalem. However, his
advisors (one always has to be careful with advisors) had
told him that if he went, he was going to be in trouble and
was going to be put in prison. Notice how Paul reacted in
Acts 21:12-14:

> And when we heard these things, both we, and they of that place,
> besought him not to go up to Jerusalem. Then Paul answered,
> What mean ye to weep and to break mine heart? for I am ready
> not to be bound only, but also to die at Jerusalem for the name
> of the Lord Jesus. And when he would not be persuaded, we
> ceased, saying, The will of the Lord be done.

Here we find men who were told, "Don't you any longer speak in the Name of Jesus." They said, "We are going
to speak in the Name of Jesus. You do whatever you want
to do. You make whatever complaints you desire. We are
going to speak in the name of Jesus!"

Paul's advisors counseled him, "Paul, if you go to Jerusalem and speak in the Name of Jesus, we already have it
from good sources that you are going to be put in prison."

Paul responded, "You break my heart! Do you mean
you are concerned that I am going to be put into prison
and bound? If God tells me to go to Jerusalem, I am not
only willing to be bound, I am also willing to be put to
death!"

God give us people of principle like Daniel, who would
pray in front of that window in spite of the fact that he
would be thrown in the lions' den.

God give us men and women of principle like young

David who was willing to go out and fight a fearsome giant because God told him to do so.

God give us people of principle like John the Baptist, who was warned that if he kept preaching repentance from sin they would have his head. Indeed, he preached against the sins of Herod and Herodias. They cut off his head and put it on a silver platter.

The government can never do away with the people of God. Even from his grave, John the Baptist preached to those people, and their consciences did them in. He preached the way of repentance. God give us men of principle who will stand for Jesus, regardless of how unpopular it might be.

Pontius Pilate had an opportunity to be a man of principle, but instead he chose popularity. If we please God, it does not matter whom we displease. If we displease God, it does not matter whom we please.

Years ago a church wanted to call my wife and me to their pastorate. It was a wonderful church. I was going to receive a $15,000-a-year raise. I was going to be given a new Lincoln automobile. I was going to have a membership in the country club.

When we visited that church, they instructed me what I could not preach on. I decided the Smiths would let them find someone who would not preach on those things. The greatest thing in the world is to be what you are for Christ, no matter where you are. It is never right to do wrong!

A man used to share with me how he would compromise and drink liquor with many of the men in order to make business deals. I remember a business deal he made that backfired on him. A Christian cannot squeeze by long with compromise. One cannot get by with wanting to be popular instead of being a person of principle.

God give us men, God give us women, God give us

teenagers of principle! Remember that line in the song "The Church Triumphant" which goes, "Men who cannot be bought and women who are above price"? Young lady, do not lower your standards for an evil-minded young man. Young man, do not try to cheat a girl out of her purity. Do not become involved in the evils of this world. Do not become a person seeking popularity instead of being a person of Christian principle.

II. Problem Two—Pilate Faced Talk Without Testimony

Not only did Pilate face popularity without principle, he also faced talk without testimony. In Matthew 27:22, I see that Pilate was trying to be a powerful talker. "What shall I do then with Jesus, which is called Christ?" He did not need to ask that question. He was a talker.

There is the kind of "dumbbell" religious person who has the attitude, "I just love Jesus, and I think the devil is not so bad either. I just think all religions are good." If one thinks all religions are good, one really does not understand what the message of Christ is all about.

Some say, "I think it is fine to be whatever you want to be, as long as you are sincere. Just believe that we are all going to heaven on many different roads. You choose one road, and I'll choose another." There is only one road to heaven, and that is the narrow road of Jesus (see Acts 4:12; John 14:6).

Beware of those who say everything is fine, wonderful, and sweet. That is exactly the conclusion Pilate had come to: I think Jesus is fine. Why should we kill Him? Then, when he was faced with Jesus, Pilate asked, "What shall I do then with Jesus, which is called Christ?" His question was unnecessary.

I do not believe you would ask that. You know what to do with Jesus! So many people want to ask questions instead of becoming busy for God. We do not need more information in our churches—we need more action! We need people to act on what they already know.

Pilate wanted to ask a question: "What shall I do then with Jesus?" Pilate knew that Jesus was innocent, that He was guilty of nothing, that He was a good man, that He was innocent of any wrongdoing. The governor knew that Jesus Christ did not deserve death. Pilate knew what he ought to do, but he implored, "What shall I do?" It was an attempt to excuse his uninvolvement and his inactivity.

People should quit asking what they are going to do with Jesus and start trusting in Him. We should start loving Him. We should start serving Him. We should give our lives to Him. We should give our money to Him. We should give our time to Him. We should give our talents to Him. We should give our all to Him. We do not need to ask, "What? Is Jesus God? Is Jesus real? Is Jesus coming back?"

The Bible is true, and those answers are all in the affirmative. Jesus Christ is the Son of God who died on Calvary. We need to quit playing games and become busy serving, loving, and trusting Jesus. Then we can watch Jesus make an impact on this lost, dead, dying world. Beware of those who are always asking, "What are we going to do about Jesus?"

You do not need more information; you need more courage to act on what you already know. Quit blaming your inactivity on your wife or your children or your job or your circumstances. The fact is, you may not love God enough to do what He wants you to do. You may presently have a talk instead of a testimony.

If you would stand up for God and be the spiritual leader you ought to be, chances are your wife and children would follow you. If they do not, God will take care of them. You stand up for God like you ought. Do what

He wants you to do. Be the man He has called you to be. Be the woman. Be the youth. Be the spiritual leader of your home. Quit your talk and start having a testimony.

Pilate was good at talking, "Oh, I think Jesus is fine. What shall I do with Him?" He knew what to do! "What shall I do with Him?" He should have set Him free. I challenge you to set Christ free in your marriage. Set Christ free to raise your children as they ought to be raised. Set Christ free in your soul-winning. Set Christ free in your giving. Set Christ free in your Christian living. Set Christ free in your day-to-day life.

Give Christ full reign of your business, and then watch miracles occur as you find Christ to be the best business partner you could ever have. Quit asking what you are going to do with Jesus Christ and just set Him free! Christ deserves your best, your all. He died for you. You know that Jesus is coming again. We do not need more information; we merely need to live according to what we already know.

Be careful of those who have talk without testimony. Pilate was good at his compliments. However, Jesus does not want your compliments. He wants your life!

III.   Problem Three—Pilate Faces Guilt Without Grief

Pilate faced not only popularity without principle and talk without testimony but a third problem as well: guilt without grief. That was a serious problem. He was guilty, yet he had no sense of guilt. As I have read the record of Pilate's situation, what stands out is this: Pilate had no sense of personal condemnation.

We find no self-abnegation in this incident. Pilate does not go off grieving. We do not find Pilate wallowing in pity, grief, and remorse. We do not hear Pilate saying, "Oh! What have I done? What have I done? What have I done?" We do not discover him saying, "I have shed the blood of an innocent man!" No! We find no words such as these coming from the mouth of Pilate.

Why? He had lived as a compromiser uncommitted to any principle or conviction. He had carved out for himself a niche of compromise, to the extent that nothing ever drew at his conscience. Pilate's conscience had become so seared by compromise and the desire for popularity and acceptance, he could do almost anything and feel no guilt.

One of the most serious times of our lives is when we become comfortable and at ease with our sins. As long as we can he lackadaisical in our church attendance with it not bothering us, we are in trouble. When we come to where we have a little pet sin which we stroke and keep clutched close to our hearts and it no longer bothers us, we are in serious trouble.

As long as your sins keep you up at night, put a little grey on your temples, etch a few furrows on your brow, make you come down the aisle and weep and fall on your face at the altar, and get to your heart and burden you—then there is hope for you! But when one discovers that he is guilty but has no sense of guilt, he is in deadly peril.

I find people all the time who say, "Preacher, that is all well and good for those who need religion. However, Preacher, I am unusually educated. I have graduated from the University of Whatever. I am not one of those weaklings like you and other people. I do not need a God to lean on. I am a self-made man. I pull myself up by my old boot straps. Really, Preacher, I do not need anybody else. I do not need a God or a Bible or a religion or a deity to lean upon to motivate me. I am what I am within myself."

What you do not understand, if words like that ever come out of your mouth, is that you are the most desperately lost of all! People who are guilty and feel guilt have a chance. There is hope for them. However, a person who is guilty and has no sense of remorse is bad off.

I have known many people who have died of a heart attack, yet had never known they had any heart trouble. I have known people who went to a doctor and discovered they had had cancer for six months. For six months the cancer had been destroying their bodies, yet they were not aware of it. I have known people who died in airplane crashes, yet who had absolutely no fear of flying.

One might remark, "I don't fear hell, and I don't want heaven. I don't have a need of the Word of God. I don't need to hear choirs sing, and I don't need to hear preachers preach. That is why I stay home on Sunday morning drinking this cup of coffee and smoking this cigarette, cussing at my wife and kids. I don't need God, the church, and the Bible!"

You may not feel a need but you have a dire one! You may not want to go to hell—you may not even believe in it—but you are going to go to hell if you do not give your heart to Christ. Merely because one does not sense a need does not mean the need does not exist.

Many people have need of medical care this minute but are not aware of it. Pilate felt no need. He was guilty without any sense of guilt: no sense of grief, never remorseful, never burdened.

A friend of mine drove up after an accident. It almost made him sick when he saw the school bus turned perpendicular to the road. He stopped his car, went around the back of the school bus, and saw a sight he wished he had never seen. A woman's car had been hit broadside by the school bus. She had been thrown out of her car. The two back tires of the school bus had run over her chest and her face. My friend reported it was a bloody, horrible sight of mangled flesh. He was the first or second person there, so he started directing traffic. About that time, the woman who had been driving the school bus walked up to him. She looked down at the dead woman who had left three little children without a mother or a father. She had been a single parent trying to raise the children by herself. Looking down at the woman she had just run over, the bus driver blurted out, "Well, that fool got what she deserved! She pulled out in front of me!"

My friend could not imagine such callous disregard for human life. Quite a few people began to gather. He thought it was strange when all of a sudden an ice-cream wagon pulled up. The ice-cream man saw a bonanza for business, so he brought the ice-cream wagon over to sell ice cream to the people watching the dead woman bleed on the pavement. Somebody offered to buy my friend an ice-cream cone, and he said, "No, I don't think I will even be able to eat supper tonight, much less ice cream."

The ambulance drove up, and the attendants scooped up that woman's bloody body to put her into the ambulance. My friend said he would never forget the sight of men gawking at that woman while they licked their popsicles over her dead body.

There are people all over this world who have that same casual attitude about Jesus. They go on their merry way, not caring one whit that He died for them. It does not bother them. They do not care. "Preacher, sweat. Turn red in the face. Scream. Hold up the Word of God! Do whatever you want, but we are going out to eat at the cafeteria if you will just shut up! We don't give a rip what Jesus did!"

You may say, "Preacher, that's callous." Yes, it is callous but also true. It is time we started caring. It is about time we started being less than casual about what Jesus did on the Cross. You are guilty of the death of Christ, whether or not you feel guilty.

If you have never trusted Jesus as your Lord and Savior,

then today is the time to give your life to Christ. If you feel no need of Christ, you are especially in need of Christ. You are horribly lost. You are without hope unless Jesus is in your life.

IV. Problem Four—Pilate Faced Ritual Without Reality

Pilate faced not only popularity without principle, talk without testimony, and guilt without grief, but there was a fourth problem as well: ritual without reality.

In Matthew 27:24 Pilate took a basin of water and began to wash his hands and to fling the water off the tips of his fingers before the multitude: "You want Jesus to be crucified? I do not, so I am letting you be responsible for it. I am washing my hands of this matter! I want you to know that I will have none of the blame for the death of Jesus upon my hands! See ye to it. It is your responsibility." So Pilate went through the ritual of washing his hands.

The ritual will not excuse you of the reality. The reality was the fact that Pilate had not done what he could. The reality was that Pilate was to blame for his indecision.

Jesus said, "You cannot be neutral. You are either for Me or are against Me. You either make Me live, or you make Me die. You either gather with Me, or you scatter abroad" (see Matt. 12:30). You do not have a choice of being neutral. To be neutral is to be negative; to be neutral is to be against Christ. If you are not aggressively for Jesus, then you are aggressively against Him. There is no neutrality.

A ritual will not excuse us of the reality. In so many churches, Sunday after Sunday, service after service, people go to church, and all they have is ritual. Like Pontius Pilate, they wash their little hands of guilt. They have a communion service, but they are only washing their hands. They have a baptismal service, but they are simply washing their hands. They have a wonderful talent show for Christ, but they are washing their hands. They are doing a ritual.

If all the church choir does is dress up in their sanctimonious robes and sing ecclesiastical songs, then the service is a farce. I believe that every word in the Bible is the inerrant, infallible Word of God.

I want you to know that I preach a real Jesus who died on a real Cross: a real Jesus who helps us to escape a real burning lake of fire, a real Jesus who prepares for us a real home in heaven with real streets of gold and a real gate of pearl, a real Jesus who gives to you a real, wonderful, eternal life. I want you to know the Holy Spirit is real and what Jesus has done in my heart is real. I do not need a mere ritual!

You do not need a preacher who plays sermonic games with you. You do not need a priest to go to in some confessional. You do not need songs of praise if they are meaningless. God is real! Jesus is real! The Holy Spirit is real! The second coming is real! You need to believe it! *It is real!*

Pilate's problem was that he had the ritual of forgiveness, but he did not know the reality of forgiveness. His heart had never been changed.

Some of you have gone through the ritual of coming down an aisle, the ritual of being baptized as a baby, the ritual of being baptized as an evangelical. Yet you have never had the reality of Christ in your heart! I feel sorry for people who go to church where the preaching and the life are just not real.

Americans will join anything if someone gives them a button and a plastic card. We have had people join churches and religious institutions and lodges. They do the ritual, but they have forgotten the reality. Jesus is real!

Some say, "It is not real to me." It may not be, but it can

be. It can be because Jesus died for you. A college play that touched my heart so much showed a scene of a home in Jerusalem during the time of Christ. When the curtain opened, one could see the mother and the father. The man happened to be a carpenter who lived during the time of the Lord Jesus Christ. The woman was talking to her husband as their two children were busy playing. The woman said, "Honey, I heard at the market today that the Roman government is advertising for carpenters to make a bid on crosses that they use for execution. Honey, you know that we have been needing some extra spending money. I know you have been making these cabinets and these chairs, but you could start making crosses and earn us some extra money."

He replied, "No, Dear, I love my work, and I love to help people to have cabinets and stools and chairs, but I just can't make a cross."

Then her pleading turned to nagging. "Well, I don't have enough spending money . . ." All of a sudden the scene faded, and the curtain opened again to another scene several weeks later.

Coming into that same house, a little boy was crying, "Mom and Dad! Mom and Dad!"

"Son, what is wrong?"

"Oh, Mom! Oh, Dad!"

"Son, what is wrong? Control yourself!"

"Mom and Dad, I was at the market, and coming down the street I saw a big crowd, and Mom and Dad, I went over there, and I saw Jesus."

"Well, Son, do you mean the Jesus that we have loved? The Jesus that we have always thought was a good man, who taught good things?"

"Yes, sir! Yes, sir! That's the man! Jesus! Jesus! Yes, Daddy, I saw Him, and, Daddy, He was carrying our Cross, a Cross that we made right out here in our shop! We made the Cross that Jesus was carrying! They are going to kill Jesus on the Cross we made!"

"No, Son. You know that there are other people who have made crosses. That was not our Cross."

"Oh, Daddy, it is our Cross! The Cross that we made right here in our shop!"

"Son! Son, calm down. Son, how do you know?"

"Daddy, do you remember when that man came by and wanted you to build cabinets?"

"Yes, Son, I remember"

"Do you remember when you and that man started talking in the living room?"

"Yes, Son."

"Daddy, I went out into the shop where we had left that cross we had just finished. I looked at the pretty Cross that we had made, and, Daddy, I did what so many famous people do—I put my name on that cross. Daddy, I did not tell you that I wrote my name on that cross. Daddy, as I was in that great crowd of people today, I saw Jesus coming by. Just when Jesus got even with me, He fell, and that Cross we had made crushed His shoulders. Daddy, I know it was our Cross because when Jesus fell right at my feet, I looked on that Cross, and there was my name! There was my name that I had put there!" The boy straightened himself up and said, "Daddy, do you understand what I am saying? My name was on that Cross!"

Ladies and gentlemen, your name and my name were on that Cross. Thank God, my name was on that Cross!

4

The Words Jesus Spoke from the Cross—I

Then said Jesus, Father, forgive them; for they know not what they do. And they parted his raiment, and cast lots. And the people stood beholding. And the rulers also with them derided him, saying, He saved others; let him save himself, if he be Christ, the chosen of God. And the soldiers also mocked him, coming to him, and offering him vinegar. And saying, If thou be the king of the Jews, save thyself. And a superscription also was written over him in letters of Greek, and Latin, and Hebrew, THIS IS THE KING OF THE JEWS. And one of the malefactors which were hanged railed on him, saying, If thou be Christ, save thyself and us. But the other answering rebuked him, saying, Dost not thou fear God, seeing thou art in the same condemnation? And we indeed justly; for we receive the due reward of our deeds: but this man hath done nothing amiss. And he said unto Jesus, Lord, remember me when thou comest into thy kingdom. And Jesus said unto him, Verily I say unto thee, Today shalt thou be with me in paradise (Luke 23:34-43).

Now there stood by the cross of Jesus his mother, and his mother's sister, Mary the wife of Cleophas, and Mary Magdalene. When Jesus therefore saw his mother, and the disciple standing by, whom he loved, he saith unto his mother, Woman, behold they son! Then saith he to the disciple, Behold thy mother! And from that hour that disciple took her unto his own home (John 19:25-27).

Many times when someone has departed this life, the question will come, "Did he say anything before he died?"

Voltaire was a French atheist who predicted the demise of Christianity. However, as he was dying, Voltaire screamed, "I have been a fool! The hell that I never believed in now awaits me!"

Robert Ingersoll, the renowned atheist, lamented, "I have lived a wasted life. I am about to leap into the dark unknown."

I heard about a man who had always been stingy in the operation of his restaurants. He was more interested in trying to make money than in serving good food. He was mumbling shortly before he died. The family leaned over to hear his profound words as he gasped, "Slice the ham thin!" He had lived trying to get by on as little as possible.

I think my favorite is not the last words of these men but rather the last will and testament of a wealthy man whose family was gathered together to hear the reading of the will. It was read by the attorney while the family sat around the room trying to look sad.

The attorney read, "I, —— ——, having made a large fortune, being of a sound mind and of proper judgment, want to reveal to my family that I spent it all!" That might be the best way to go.

Christians also die the way they live. I will never forget having read the last words of William Carey, the great missionary: "When I am gone, speak less of Carey and more of Carey's Savior."

Susanna Wesley was the mother of John and Charles Wesley, the founders of Methodism. Knowing that she had only a few hours to live, Susanna Wesley exulted,

"Children! Children! I am about ready to go be with our Lord. Would you please sing a song of praise to God?" What a way to end a life!

Adoniram Judson testified, "I do not dislike this world. I have enjoyed my ministry and my work for Christ. Now I am leaving this world and going to heaven with the same attitude as that of a young boy leaving school heading for the playground. I am going to heaven the same way!" What a spirit! What a joy when one nears the end of one's life in expectation and anticipation for heaven that is yet to come.

As we look at the crucifixion of the Lord Jesus Christ, we might ask the same question, "Did He say anything before He died?" The answer, indeed, is *yes!* Jesus spoke significant and glorious words. As He neared the end of His earthly life, Jesus spoke seven "words" from the Cross. In this message, we are going to look at the first three "words" Jesus spoke from the Cross.

I. A Word of Intercession

The first word was one of intercession. He gazed down from that Cross after His enemies had crucified Him and, in a word of interceding prayer, prayed, "Father, forgive them; for they know not what they do" (Luke 23:34). I want you to notice three facts about that word of intercession.

A. A Word of Prophecy

First of all, notice that it was a word of prophecy. In Isaiah 53:12 is recorded a great prophetic truth, one of many in Isaiah 53 that tells about Jesus' death. "Therefore will I divide him a portion with the great, and he shall divide the spoil with the strong; because he hath poured out his soul unto death: and he was numbered with the transgressors; and he bare the sin of many, and made intercession for the transgressors" (v. 12).

Here Jesus was praying for some people who would not have been prayed for had He not been willing to do it. They had crucified Him, yet Jesus said, "Nobody takes my life from me; I lay it down freely for those that I love" (see John 10:18). Hebrews 7:25 declared, "[Christ] ever liveth to make intercession for them."

He is the interceding Lord. From the very beginning it was prophesied that He would die interceding in prayer for transgressors. He is still at the right hand of the Father. He is still making intercession for us. He not only interceded for His enemies while on the Cross, He is still interceding for those who will receive Him and want to know His Father.

In Luke 23:34, Jesus prayed, "Father, forgive them; for they know not what they do." It is the same term that Simon Peter used in Acts 3:17 as he preached on the Day of Pentecost. Peter said to those Jewish leaders, "I [know] that through ignorance ye [have crucified the Son of God]." The word *ignorance* is a derivation of the term Jesus used when He prayed, "They know not what they do." Literally, what Jesus said was, "Father, forgive their ignorance."

When I realize that what Jesus prayed for from the Cross was the same concept Simon Peter preached on the Day of Pentecost, then I understand why Pentecost was such a fruitful harvest. Three thousand souls were not saved as a result of the powerful preaching of Peter; rather, they were saved because of the powerful praying of Jesus! It was not in response to the preaching of Peter. It was the answer of the Father in heaven to the prayer of His Son on the Cross! "Father, forgive these who crucify Me. Bring them to a moment of repentance, to salvation, to a moment of awareness, to a moment where they might understand that they have crucified the Son of God."

It is thrilling to know that today Christ is still praying for you and for me; He is praying for our repentance; He is praying for revival in our hearts; He is praying for our churches. He is interceding in every way to the Father that the blessings of heaven might rain upon us in abundance.

It was a prayer, then, of prophetic truth. It was prophesied in Isaiah 53:12 that there would be a word of prophecy from the Cross, A word of prophecy that was fulfilled on the Day of Pentecost when three thousand were saved as a result of Jesus' praying, "Father, forgive them; for they know not what they do."

B. A Word of Prayer

Not only was Christ's first word from the Cross one of prophecy, it was also a word of prayer. As a man is about to die, sometimes his attitude gets bitter. You remember Samson. Samson was taken by his enemies, blinded, and bound in chains. Time passed, and his hair began to grow again. Thus, his strength began to return. One day they chained Samson, that mighty man, between the pillars of the pagan temple. With his dying breath, he flexed those strong muscles and began to pull at the chains. He broke down the pillars of the temple.

As the mortar and stones of that pagan temple caved in, Samson and his enemies were crushed to death.

Consider Stephen at the time of his death. Some say that bitterness certainly was not the attitude of Stephen since he said, "Father, forgive those that stone me. Forgive those that take my life." However the difference is that, first of all, Stephen said, "Lord Jesus, receive my spirit" (Acts 7:59). Then he prayed for the Father to forgive them. Jesus did not pray, "Father, into thy hands I commend my spirit" first. First He offered a prayer unto the Father that the Father might forgive His killers.

Jesus did not say, "I forgive them." He said, "Father, I want you to do it. I want you to forgive them."

In Matthew 5:44, when Jesus was telling us how to be Christians, He didn't say, "Forgive your enemies." What Jesus said was, "Love your enemies."

There is a significant passage on the subject of forgiveness and pardoning in Luke 17:3-4:

> Take heed to yourselves: If thy brother trespass against thee, rebuke him; and if he repent, forgive him. And if he trespass against theee seven times in a day, and seven times in a day turn again to thee, saying, I repent; thou shalt forgive him."

In Matthew 18:22, Jesus taught that we are to forgive seventy times seven.

However, it is interesting in Matthew 18:15 that Jesus encouraged us to do two things before granting forgiveness. Number one, we are to rebuke the person. Number two, we are to expect them to say, "I am sorry, and to the best of my ability I will not do it anymore." That is called repentance. Rebuke them, and expect them to repent. Then you are to forgive them.

Some may ask, "What about the example of Jesus in the Model Prayer when He taught that we are to forgive our debtors?" (Matt. 6:12). Don't you remember the example shortly before that where Jesus instructed the Christians to make a petititon to the Father in heaven to "forgive us our debts, as we forgive our debtors"? What is He saying to us? Do not expect people to forgive you if you have not repented! You have no right to expect forgiveness unless, first of all, you have been willing to be chastened, and, secondly, you have been willing to repent.

Jesus laid down these principles from His own lips: if someone has sinned against you or if someone has gone opposite the Word of God, they must be rebuked, and, secondly, they must be willing to turn from their sin, to repent.

As far as I know there is no reference in the Bible where God ever forgave a sinner who did not repent. There must be the matter of turning from sin. There must be remorse and contrition! There must be a spirit of penitence, saying, "Lord, I am sorry for what I have done. I am willing to change."

Someone may say, "Hot dog! I've been wanting to be bitter for years. Now here is my chance. There is someone I have been wanting to hold a grudge against, and now Bailey Smith says it is all right!" What am I saying? Before you expect forgiveness from someone, Jesus emphasizes that they have a right to tell you that you have hurt them, and, second, the Bible expects you to repent.

So many people want to live in evil and then wonder why the world does not run to their doorsteps in love. It is not scriptural to do so. The problem in "easy forgiveness" is that it seems to condone a life-style with which God Himself is not pleased. Some of us have had "easy forgiveness" on our lips, but it has always backfired because it encourages a person to continue in their evil and in their unrepentant spirit. God does not encourage that kind of forgiveness.

As far as we know, Jesus did not forgive His murderers, even though He was willing. Those who crucified Him were not forgiven until they repented of what they had done and accepted Christ on the Day of Pentecost. There was a spirit of pardon. There was a prayer: "Father, I want You to forgive them."

C. A Word of Pardon

There is a word of prophecy and a word of prayer. As

we continue to look at Jesus' word of intercession from the Cross, there is now a word of pardon.

"Father, forgive them; for they know not what they do." The Bible says in Romans 4:8, "Blessed is the man to whom the Lord will not impute sin." Colossians 2:13 says, "You . . . hath he quickened together with him, having forgiven you all trespasses." Colossians 3:3, "For ye are dead, and your life is hid with Christ in God."

Now *God formed* you, *sin deformed* you, and *Christ transformed* you. When you understand that process, you understand what God is going to do with you as it relates to pardon.

Years ago, I was in Vallejo, California, a little city across the bay from San Francisco. One day the pastor and I visited a certain man. He was almost to the point of repentance and confession when he raised an interesting question: "Mr. Smith, I can repent of my sins, and I can believe that Christ will save me. However, I have never been able to understand what preachers mean when they say that Christ will also forgive the sins I have yet to commit. I don't understand how He can forgive sins that I haven't yet committed. How can He forgive sins I am going to commit in the future?"

He looked at me as if to say, "Buddy, I have buffaloed you!" After a pause of only a few seconds, I came back with, "Let me ask you something. How many of your sins were future at the time Jesus died on the Cross?" A big smile crossed his face, and he said, "A hundred percent." I said, "That's right, 'A hundred percent.' All of them. Every sin you would ever commit was in the future when Jesus died for them!"

Aren't you glad that when the Bible talks about the forgiveness of your sins, it is past, it is present, and it is future! Every sin that we would ever commit was in the future from the time that Jesus Christ died on the Cross.

He knew what we were going to do. He knew our evil. He knew our drunkenness. He knew our fornication. He knew our lying. He knew our cheating. He knew all of our shortcomings.

In spite of the fact that He knew all of that so vividly, He pardoned us and forgave us of those sins. He does not impute to us the life of sin. He imputes to us the life of righteousness. What does "impute" mean? It means that when God the Father looks at us, He does not see us as lost sinners; He sees us as persons who have had their sins washed away by the blood of Christ. He sees us through what Jesus did on the Cross. What a blessed truth!

Perhaps you are thinking, *I do not deserve that.* No, you do not deserve it, and neither do I! Yet God does not see me as a dirty, filthy, rotten sinner. He sees me as one that has been made clean, pure, and righteous through what Jesus did upon the Cross. And He sees you in the righteousness of Christ.

Praise God for this word of intercession. It is a word of prophecy; it is a word of prayer; it is a word of pardon. God forgave on the Day of Pentecost because the people were willing to repent.

II. A Word of Inspiration

Jesus looked down from the Cross and prayed, "Father, forgive them; for they know not what they do" (Luke 23:34). Then He also gave a word of inspiration.

There were two thieves crucified with our Lord, one on either side. One man "railed on Him," the other man wanted forgiveness (v. 39).

I told our architect that on the top of our new church building, I wanted three crosses. He asked, "How about one?" I answered, "Since I pay the bills, how about three?" He relented, "All right, three, but I have never seen a church with three crosses." An evangelistic church needs to see all three crosses. On the cross on Jesus' left, a man died in sin, rejecting Christ. On the cross on Jesus' right, a man died to sin, praying, "Lord, remember me when thou comest into thy kingdom" (v. 42). On the center Cross, a Man died for sin.

What a beautiful story! The three crosses tell about the redeeming power of the Lord Jesus Christ. Not only did Christ give from the Cross a word of intercession, interceding on behalf of his enemies, He also gave a word of inspiration to that thief. Jesus said to him, "To-day shalt thou be with me in paradise" (v. 43).

I cannot imagine a more telling illustration of the grace of God and the human free will than the story of the other two crosses. For instance, why did the man on the left reject Christ and the man on the right receive Him? I do not know. Both of them had a horrible background. Both of them were bleeding. Both of them were going to have their limbs broken. Both of them were going to die upon those crosses. Both of them had been political rebels and thieves.

Why could one be so bitter as to reject Christ and one be so humble as to receive Him? How do you explain that? I believe that the secret to understanding why some people reject Christ and why some people receive Christ involves the concept of acknowledgment. I learned in twenty-six years of being a pastor, that if people will acknowledge their sins and their needs, then one can help them to understand the place and the power of Jesus. It all depends on whether or not they come to the place of acknowledgment.

The old saying is: You must get people lost before you can get them saved. As long as people are cocky and arrogant, thinking that their sins are OK, they mistakenly believe that God approves of their errors and their evil. Since they think God approves of the way they are living, they will never change; they will never repent. Therefore, God will never forgive them. They will never have a new life. They will never be born again. They will never escape hell and make heaven. They will never know the joys of eternal life. As long as they excuse their sins, there is no hope.

One man on the cross looked over and snorted, "Ha! Man, if you are the King of the Jews, save yourself and us at the same time." The other thief came to the defense of Jesus. He protested, "Now, wait a minute. He has not done anything wrong, but you have! You are in pretty bad shape to start blaming God."

I have always thought it strange that people one heartbeat from hell would, all of a sudden, start finding fault in churches or in preachers. They are in no position to be critical. They are in no position to be cranky. They are held by a thin thread out of the lake of fire. Do people not know that the second coming of Christ is near, and they are going to be standing at the judgment bar of God?

Some may have a really difficult time in believing the doctrine of election, but we ought to thank God that we are believers. Ponder that for a moment. Why in the world do you believe, and that good old boy around the corner does not? Why do you drink soft drinks, and others booze it up? Why do you live decently, and some other people do not?

I do not know why? I do not understand why I am the way I am. I do not know why I believe in the Bible. I do not know why Jesus has saved me and the Holy Spirit has indwelt me. I do not know why my dad used to drive a fire truck and a streetcar in Dallas, Texas. I do not know why God suddenly saved him and called him to preach, though he never finished high school. However, I certainly am joyful that somehow my dad became a believer, my mom became a believer, and I became a believer!

I could have been a rebel. I could have been a smart-aleck lost man. I could have been some old heathen, but I am not one! Praise God that for some reason, in the elective power of the grace of God, I am a believer. I am in church. I am not a rebel. I am not a God hater. I am not a Christ denier. It is no credit to me. It is only by the wonderful grace of God.

Reader, look at yourself. You are a believer through no credit of your own. It is because God loves you and chose you for salvation. Through His grace, He elected you and made you a believer. Praise God for that!

The thief on the right was a believer. The thief on the left was a rejector. Why? I do not know!

I read one of Charles Haddon Spurgeon's sermons in order to receive a little bit of help on the matter of election. Spurgeon was undoubtedly one of the greatest preachers who ever lived. If anyone would be able to correlate divine election and the free will of man, it would have to be Spurgeon. Spurgeon's comment on 1 Timothy 2:3-4, where the Bible says that God "will have all men to be saved," is:

> There stands the text, and I believe that it is my Father's wish that all men should be saved and come to the knowledge of the truth. But, I also know that He does not will it. So that He will not save any one of them unless they believe in His Son. For He has told us over and over again, He will not. He will not save any man except he forsakes his sin and turns to Him with full purpose of heart. That I also know, and I also know that He has people whom He will save, whom by His eternal love, He has chosen. Whom, by His eternal power, He will deliver. I do not know how that squares with this Scripture. That is another of the things that I do not know.

I finished that sermon, and I said, "Thanks a lot, Spurgeon!" All he did say was, "That is another of the things

I do not know!" It was as if he looked up from the page and quipped, "Smith, I did not help you one bit."

It is God's elective grace. You say you do not understand it. Good! If you do understand it, you are incorrect. God chooses everyone who is born again. Do not ever say that you do not believe it. You have to believe it because that is what the Bible says.

Perhaps you are thinking, *Well! I do not believe God chooses anyone to go to hell.* That is right! God never chooses anyone to go to hell. He does not want anyone to go to hell (see 1 Pet. 3:9). He wants everyone to be saved. However, those who are saved, God has chosen before the foundation of the earth. Like Spurgeon, you and I may not understand it. Yet divine election is a wonderful, glorious truth. God chose you to be saved.

Consider two different men whom God saved. One man was named Saul of Tarsus. He was punctilious in his desire to keep the Law. He was rigid. He dotted every *i* and crossed every *t*. Saul even referred to himself as "a Hebrew of the Hebrews" and "a Pharisee of the Pharisees."

The other man was one thief on the cross. He never kept the Law. He probably hated the Law. He was a rebel against the Law. He was a criminal against the Law.

Saul of Tarsus had a background of always keeping every part of the Law. When he was converted, Paul became the most loyal Christian who ever lived. He wrote much of the New Testament. He served the Lord gladly. He was stoned, beaten, threatened, shipwrecked, and eventually martyred for the Lord. Every day, with his hands he labored for God. Every day his feet carried him into Lystra or Iconium or Derbe or some other place where he preached the gospel of Christ.

The other man never served God one moment. The thief on the cross never used his hands for God because they were nailed to the cross. He never moved his feet down a dusty road in order to witness for Jesus. Why? They had a huge spike through them, and he could not move them.

One man tried never to break the law; one man never kept the law. One man, after he was saved, used his life for Christ. One man, after he was saved, never did one thing for Christ. He couldn't. Yet both men went to heaven because of the grace of our loving God who chose them both. God, in His divine grace, may save people of totally different backgrounds and totally different futures. They are both equally saved by the grace of God! When we see this wonderful word of inspiration, we view how gloriously God is working out His plan and purpose in so many areas of our lives.

After the church service once a man confessed to me, "I owe you an apology." I asked, "Why do you owe me an apology?"

He explained: "Aren't you coming to Fort Smith, Arkansas, to preach an area-wide crusade?" Yes, I was.

"I knew you were. In fact, I have already told my wife that I had heard one of your tapes, and I was not going to go hear you preach."

"Really."

"Yes, I told my wife I was not going to go to hear that man." (In fact, they had already made arrangements to be out of town that week while I was in Fort Smith.) "Then I came here to Russellville today for a job interview. I got in late, and my boss said to me, 'We don't have time to talk right now. I go up here to First Baptist Church. If you will go to church with me, we will go out to eat and talk after the service.' " He capped it off: "Low and behold, I got here, and Bailey Smith was preaching!" You know what happened?—he was saved!

In the elective, searching, seeking process of God, He

is going to save people of every kind of walk of life. They are going to be wonderfully saved, and God is going to perform His will in their lives. Jesus turned toward the thief on His right when that thief requested, "Lord, remember me when thou comest into thy kingdom." Jesus promised, "To-day shalt thou be with me in paradise."

Jesus reassured all of us, "In my Father's house are many mansions: if it were not so, I would have told you. I go to prepare a place for you. . . . that where I am, there ye may be also" (John 14:2-3). If Jesus is there, it is heaven!

First Thessalonians 4:16-17 says that "the Lord himself shall descend from heaven with a shout, with the voice of the archangel, and with the trump of God: and the dead in Christ shall rise first: Then we, which are alive and remain shall be caught up together with them in the clouds, to meet the Lord in the air: and so shall we ever be with the Lord"!

How marvelous it will be to walk down the street and kick up gold dust! How fantastic it will be to enter a gate of pearl and sit down with Mom and Dad you have loved and lost temporarily! How great it will be to live eternally on Hallelujah Boulevard and walk by those gorgeous streams in that Celestial City! As great as all that is, the greatest fact is that we have the promise of Jesus' being there! "To-day shalt thou be with me in paradise"!

But what is paradise? Heaven! I know about Christ preaching in prison, but I can prove to you that paradise is the same as heaven. In 2 Corinthians 12:2, Paul is talking about his own rapture experience: "I knew a man in Christ above fourteen years ago, (whether in the body, I cannot tell; or whether out of the body, I cannot tell: God knoweth;) such an one caught up to the third heaven." The first heaven is where the clouds are. The second heaven is where the stars are. The third heaven is where the redeemed, the born-again people, are in the presence of God.

Paul continued in verses 3-4*a*, "And I knew such a man, (whether in the body, or out of the body, I cannot tell: God knoweth;) How that he was caught up into paradise." "Paradise" in verse 4 is the same word as "heaven" in verse 2.

Revelation 2:7 refers to the tree of life being in paradise. Revelation 22:2 says that the tree of life is in the New Jerusalem. I believe paradise and the New Jerusalem are one and the same. I know about the "bosom of Abraham," the Old Testament representation of heaven, and I know about hades. But that thief went to be with Christ in heaven! There is no soul sleep.

When you put your mom, if she were a born-again Christian, out there in a lonely cemetery, she was not going to stay in that grave until the resurrection. Her last breath on this earth merged into her first breath in heaven.

There is no soul sleep! Never ever believe those who teach it. There is no purgatory. There is no body limbo. To be absent from the body is to be present with the Lord. Jesus said, "To-day shalt thou be with me in paradise." The Word of God affirms that when we die in Jesus we go to be with Him. We go to be with Him forever and forever in that glorious city called the New Jerusalem, the holy city, heaven, paradise. Indeed it is a paradise.

III. A Word of Interest

From the Cross, Jesus not only spoke a word of intercession and a word of inspiration, but also a word of interest. In John 19:26-27, Jesus looked down at His mother and His beloved disciple John. He said, "Woman, behold thy son! . . . Behold thy mother!" What I want you to see from this word is: Jesus, in a time of excruciating pain and dreadful agony, cared for His mother, "Mother, take care of My brother, and Brother, take care of My mother."

When we are committed to Christ, nothing derails us. Nothing should upset us. I am amazed at people who get upset and want to quit God and quit church. They are spoiled, thinking only about themselves! They need to become obsessed with the things of God.

I heard about a counselor writing about a woman who was repeatedly feeling depressed and defeated. He asked the woman to make a list of why she felt defeated. She brought back a typewritten piece of paper she had entitled "My Reasons for Defeat."

I clipped out the counselor's report, and here is part of what the woman had written: "I am unhappy and dissatisfied with life. I doubt myself and my ambitions. I worry about many things. I am afraid of emotions. I worry about unpaid bills. I am troubled abut what people say or think. I am always lonely. I worry about my failures and mistakes, past and to come. I am anxious about my health. I am afraid of losing my mind. I fear the future. I worry about the possibility of becoming an invalid. I am always blue and discouraged. I doubt my few spiritual high moments. I do not have real spiritual peace. I am always defeated." Need I go on?

Do you see her problem? She has an *I* problem. She needs to see the *I* doctor. His name is Dr. Jesus. If you will go to Dr. Jesus, you will quit talking about *I*.

I thought of this, and I compared the story of William Booth who founded the Salvation Army. When he was taken to the hospital, his son Bramwell, leaned over his bed and said, "Father, the doctors said that when you take off the bandages, you are going to be blind." William Booth turned toward his son and expressed his heart, "Son, don't you fret about that. God has used this old body to help the poor and to help the work of Jesus with eyes.

Now, God is going to use this old body to help the poor and the work of Jesus without eyes." There was a joyful man. He lost himself in the spirit of his work.

When Jesus was on the Cross dying for humankind, He had time to look down and help His mother and a friend. When one is committed to Jesus, to the cause of soul-winning, and to the cause of redemption, nothing derails him. Nothing discourages him. Nothing makes him mad. He does not have a chip on his shoulder. He does not bristle. He does not allow somebody to hurt his feelings.

One is so busy for Jesus that nothing else matters. One has work to do. One is involved in meeting the needs of those around him. Jesus was in indescribable agony and pain, yet He had time to be concerned about others. Why? That is what He was: a man concerned about others. Lose your life in the work of Jesus, and you will not have time to hurt like you have been hurting. Center your life in Jesus and His work.

5

The Words Jesus Spoke
from the Cross—II

Now from the sixth hour there was darkness over all the land unto the ninth hour (Matt. 27:45).

In the previous chapter we looked at the word of *intercession*, the first word Jesus spoke from the Cross. Jesus said, "Father, forgive them; for they know not what they do" (Luke 23:34). Jesus did not forgive them at that moment because they could not be forgiven until they repented and committed their lives to Him.

The second word was a one of *inspiration*. Jesus said to that penitent thief, "To-day shalt thou be with me in paradise" (Luke 23:43).

The third one was the word of *interest*. Even at the most crucial moment of His life, Jesus had an abiding interest in others. As He hung on the Cross, Jesus spoke to His mother: "Woman, behold thy son!" (John 19:26). Then He turned to John, His beloved disciple, and said, "Behold thy Mother!" (v. 27).

Even amid His own needs, His own hurts, His own

aches, His own tormenting pain, Jesus had time to think about others.

There was a word of intercession. There was a word of inspiration. There was a word of interest. Jesus had been horribly nailed to the Cross for six hours. He had been in total darkness for the last three hours. The railing has taken place on the part of the mockers. His life was rapidly ebbing away from Him. The whole world seemed to be in confusion.

I. A Word of Isolation

Jesus spoke a fourth word from the Cross. It was a word of isolation. In that moment Jesus cried out from the Cross, "Eli, Eli, lama sabachthani?" Translated into English that means, "My God, My God, why hast thou forsaken me?" (Matt. 27:46).

Such an interesting word! In my limitations I cannot take you to the depths of its meaning. With my minor gift of rhetoric I cannot describe to you the heights of theological meaning in these words from Jesus. "Eli, Eli, lama sabachthani?" God, why have You forsaken Me?

That word *forsaken* is the Greek word *egkatelipes* which comes from the word *egkataleipō*. It means "to leave in the lurch." What Jesus said to the Father at that point is such an alarming statement. "God, how could You leave Me in the lurch? How could You leave Me without a solution? How could You leave Me without an answer? How could You leave Me in the most needful, critical moment of My life? My God! My God! Why?"

There is no other place in the Bible where Jesus asked His Father in heaven, "Why?" Never did He ask, "Why has Satan tempted Me in the wilderness?" He never implored, "Why has Judas betrayed Me? Why did Peter deny Me? Why have the disciples gone to sleep when I have told them to stay awake? Why have I been tempted for forty days?" Never!

You will discover that these words of Jesus are a direct quote from Psalm 22:1. Some have thought that in the delirium of the moment, with a high fever and in blinding pain, Jesus was not thinking properly and was merely quoting a Scripture.

I believe there is some truth to the idea that Jesus was indeed quoting a passage He had used all of His life in all of His ministry: Psalm 22. Jesus was not only quoting Scripture, He was doing far more. He was delving deeply into that very issue: "God, why have You forsaken me?"

It is a haunting idea. It is a devastating concept to imagine the Father forsaking Jesus. When I studied these seven words, I discovered an idea that is worth noting. In the very beginning of His expressions from the Cross, Jesus prayed, "Father, forgive them; for they know not what they do." Notice what He called God: "Father!" His final expression was: "Father, into thy hands I commend my spirit" (Luke 23:46).

The first word Jesus spoke from the Cross—"Father." The last word Jesus spoke from the Cross—"Father." The first word included, "Father, into Thy hands I commend my spirit."

It is interesting that every time Jesus talked to the Father from the Cross, He called Him, "Father." Except here. There is the sense in which Jesus could not see God at that moment as the Father. It was a rare matter for Jesus to call Him, "God." Even in the Garden of Gethsemane, Jesus prayed, "Father, not My will, but Thine be done." There was an intimate relationship that an only begotten Son could have with His Father. But not now. Not at this moment. Not at the word of isolation. Not at this fourth word to which we have come. Jesus does not refer to Him as His Father, but implores, "My God, My God, why hast Thou forsaken Me?"

In 2 Corinthians 5:21, Paul writes that Jesus became sin that we might become the righteousness of God through Him. The reason for this moment of isolation was that God had to hide His eyes and turn His back upon His Son as if Jesus did not exist. He became *sin* for us. So dark, so evil, so full of corruption that God the Father, in all of His holiness, could not look upon the horrible sin that Christ had become.

With all of my heart, I believe that when Jesus prayed in Gethsemane, "Father, let this cup pass from me," He was not thinking about the torment. I do not believe He meant the physical pain of the Cross. I feel that what Jesus was referring to was the fact that the Father would have to turn His back upon Him as Jesus literally became sin on the Cross in order to redeem a lost world.

It is my belief that at that moment Jesus uttered those words from hell. He did not go to hell to pay for my sin and yours at the moment He died. Rather, it was at this moment that He descended to the very depths of Satan's abode. In the very pits of hell itself, Jesus cried out, "My God, My God, why hast Thou forsaken Me?" Even though His human body resided upon the Cross, His spirit had descended to the depths of Sheol. There, in the pain that a lost man would experience for an eternity, Jesus experienced our hell and our death and our grave and our torment and our punishment for our sin. Paul expressed, "He hath made Him to be sin for us, who knew no sin; that we might be made the righteousness of God in Him." What a substitution! What a sacrifice Jesus made in our behalf!

When Jesus talked to people about hell, he referred to hell as "Gehenna." I have been to Gehenna, "the valley of Hinnom." Gehenna is the valley northeast of Jerusalem where the garbage pit was located. Today it is still a dump, even though it is far more respectable than it was in Jesus' day. When Jesus told people what hell was like, He would use an illustration. He would teach that hell is like Gehenna.

The people knew what Gehenna was. They would bring their garbage out there and set it on fire. As the fire was about to die down, some more garbage would be put on, and the fire would flame up again. That is why Jesus said, "Hell is a place where the fire never dies."

He also said hell is a place where maggots devour those decaying bodies and that decomposing trash. Jesus would say that hell is a place "where the worm dieth not and the fire is never quenched."

What did Jesus mean when He talked about hell as being a place of "weeping and wailing and gnashing of teeth"? The Jews would throw unclaimed criminals, who were sick unto death, into that garbage pit at Gehenna. The dying criminals would wail and cry out in pain. They would gargle out their last guttural sounds of life as the bitter moment of death finally came. There in Gehenna, criminals would cry out, as across the city one could hear their wails of agony and their cries for mercy, which would not be forthcoming.

Jesus also said hell is a place where there would be the "gnashing of teeth." Jesus used an example with which people were familiar. The dogs would jump into the pit and fight over the last remains of carrion. They would fight over a piece of meat, a morsel of food. The dogs' teeth would gnash at one another like sinners will gnash at one another when they are thrown into the pits of hell and torment.

That is what Jesus said hell would be like. It would be like that horrible place of decomposing bodies, of live maggots, and of unquenchable fire. Jesus experienced that kind of a place for you. He descended to that environment so you might not ever have to go there. You can escape all of that by committing yourself totally to the Lord Jesus Christ.

I want you to imagine a pit for a moment. Imagine a pit full of the most fearsome creatures of all. I am talking about a pit of vipers, snakes, poisonous spiders, scorpions. Put into that pit the putrefying dead bodies of this world. Put into that pit the oozing, diseased sores of mankind. Put into that pit all the evil deeds of mankind. If you were to mix all of that up, as if it were a cauldron of poisonous, sinister stew, and then look at that vile concoction alongside the heart of Jesus, they would look exactly the same! The Bible declares that Jesus became sin for us!

Several places in the Bible, God makes a list of sin. Galatians 5:19-21 is one of them. Here are all of those disgusting sins which the pit of sin would entail: "Adultery, fornication, uncleanness, lasciviousness, idolatry, witchcraft, hatred, variance, emulations, wrath, strife, seditions, heresies, envying, murders, drunkenness, revelings, and such like." The Bible states that Jesus became that! Jesus became that horrible combination and accumulation of all those cancerous sins.

Let me remind you that Jesus never became sinful, even though He became sin. He never sinned, but He became sin. Can you imagine the hideous cauldron of sin I have described as literally a picture of the heart of Jesus at that time? Every evil in the history of mankind; every wicked deed; every rape; every robbery; every child molestation; every dope sale; every bottle of booze that has killed an innocent family in an automobile wreck. Every dictator waging a war against innocent people—all of that Christ became! What died that day was not just the Son of God. What died on Calvary that day was the consequences of sin to those who would give their lives to Jesus. Jesus paid the price!

Jesus became sin so you might know the righteousness of God through Him. Oh! What a touching picture! What a selfless sacrifice! Jesus descended into a place like Gehenna in order that you might not have to go there. He became like you are, in order that you might become like He is. He became sin so you might become righteousness. What a story: God turned His back on His Son so He would never have to turn His back on you! Jesus was forsaken by God the Father. That is why He cried out, "My God, My God, why hast Thou forsaken Me?"

He paid the last farthing for our sin. "My God, My God, why hast Thou forsaken Me?" I thank God today for that glorious word of isolation.

In John 11:49, Caiaphas was talking about Jesus. Then in the following verse, that high priest asked, "How is it that one man would die for the people?" Caiaphas used the Greek word *huper,* translated "for." In this context, it means one who would literally stretch his body upon the body of a friend to protect him from a weapon. Caiaphas had no idea he was preaching theological truth, as he asked about Jesus, "How would one man pay the price for many men?"

Aren't you glad that Jesus stretched Himself out across you and took upon Himself the pain that you were to receive, the sword that you were to feel, the hell that awaited you, the punishment that you deserved? How in the world could anyone say "No!" to Christ. "No!" to His sacrifice. "No!" to His Cross. "No!" to His love. "No!" to His blood. "No!" to this Book?

How could anyone look at what Jesus did for them on the Cross and then claim, "I don't care"? Why would you die and do what Jesus had already done for you? Why would you do that? "Jesus paid it all, all to Him I owe."

II. A Word of Identification

Not only did Jesus speak a word of isolation, He spoke yet another word from the Cross. The fifth word was a word of identification.

In John 19:28, Jesus spoke these two words, "I thirst." It is interesting that only John recorded this word from the Cross.

Much of the New Testament was written to counteract the teachings of Gnosticism. Gnosticism was an evil doctrine of the day. As you realize, certain doctrines today are dividing churches, splitting churches, and causing churches to decay and to die. Gnosticism had to be addressed. Paul wrote many of his epistles because of the threat of Gnosticism to the churches he had founded. John grappled with the Gnostics as he wrote His Gospel and his three epistles.

Gnosticism was composed of two camps: the Docetics and the Cerinthians. The Docetics claimed that Jesus Christ never really had a physical body. Therefore, Christ could not have been material or flesh, because flesh is evil and the Son of God could not have been evil.

The Docetics taught that there were four descending levels of deity and that Jesus came from the lowest one. They were descending in value in the form of a spiral. The top level was mostly of God. The next was a little bit less of God. The third was not so much of God, and the fourth was barely deity at all.

Therefore, the Docetics came up with the heresy that Jesus had no physical body. It was only an apparition, it was only a myth, it only "appeared" to be a body. The Docetics even taught that when Jesus put His foot down upon the sand it did not leave a footprint. That teaching was prevalent in the New Testament church.

The Cerinthians, who were named after their founder,

Cerinthus, said that Christ was never actually born, nor did He actually die. They taught that Christ came into being at His baptism and that He went out of this earth before the Cross. That which was born in Bethlehem was a little human being. That which died upon the Cross was a human being. The Cerinthians said that *Christ* came upon *Jesus* at His baptism and departed from Jesus before His Cross.

I am amazed at the wild tales, which have no biblical truth, some people—even some Baptists—are believing even today! A new leader comes up with a new slant. It does not matter how dynamic he is, if what he is teaching does not fit the Bible, you ought to stay away from him! I do not care how exciting he is, how emotional he is, how intellectually stimulating he is, if what he is teaching does not jibe with the Word of God, it is a lie!

You do not need another book to add to the Bible. You do not need another man to add to Jesus. You do not need another spirit to add to the Holy Spirit. Stick to the Word of God and the Holy Trinity and to the undeniable inerrancy of this Bible, and you are going to be where God wants you to be.

So, when these Gnostics were preaching, they failed to realize that Jesus had identified with us. They could not understand, for instance, Hebrews 2:17 which says that Jesus in every way took on the form of a human being. He had all the human characteristics. Jesus was as much human as if not God, and He was as much God as if not human.

You counter with, "I don't understand that." You never will; only God understands that. Jesus was 100 percent man and 100 percent God. All man and all God. Totally man and totally God. I do not understand it. It is one of the mysteries of divine revelation, but Jesus is the God-man.

The fifth word was one of identification because when Jesus thirsted, He thirsted like we do. I studied as much as I could in regard to how long it had been since Jesus had had moisture on His lips. He best I could determine is that it had been seventeen to twenty hours since the Last Supper. Jesus had gone approximately twenty hours from the time He had drunk the cup at the Last Supper until the moment when He was dying on the Cross. I have heard of people who have lived sixty days or more without food, but one cannot live long without water.

He was needing a drink, so He cried out, "I thirst!" He identified with people who have needs, who hurt, and who ache. In mockery and derision, a Roman soldier offered Him a drink vinegar. That vinegar was not the kind with which we make salad oil. That vinegar was a sour wine so bad that even the soldiers would not drink it.

The soldier dipped a sponge into this sour wine, then squeezed it upon hyssop, which had been tied to the end of a long reed. This vinegar-soaked hyssop was placed upon the lips of Jesus who was so thirsty He drank it.

You might recall that hours earlier they had offered Jesus a sip of bitter gall, which he had refused to drink. The bitter gall contained a narcotic drug. Out of human compassion, the Roman soldiers would often give this narcotic to those being crucified in order to lessen the pain. Jesus refused the narcotic because He wanted to experience every agonizing pain for us that He could, as He bore our death, punishment, payment, and hell.

This particular passage reached out and grabbed my heart as nothing had in a long time, as I thought of the blessed Son of God dying for my sins.

He screamed out, "I thirst!" Oh, my friend, He did thirst! When Jesus was cut, He bled. When people rejected Him, it disturbed Him. He had emotions. There were times when He became righteously angry. Hebrews 2:17

reminds us that Jesus took upon Himself our characteristics. He who "thought it not robbery to be equal with God . . . took upon him the form of a servant . . . and became obedient unto death, even the death of the cross." Jesus screamed out, in essence, "I need some refreshing water." Instead of that, He got the mocking gesture of a soldier giving Him bitter, sour, overly-fermented wine. It would not quench His thirst—only make Him more thirsty.

In this passage there is another understanding for thirst. Obviously Jesus thirsted for water. What does Jesus thirst for today? Water? Oh, no. Now, one time He could have turned stones to bread for He was the Bread of Life, but He did not do it. Why? He waited for someone to bring Him bread. Jesus could have caused a cup of cool water to appear in the clouds, be poured upon His lips, but no. He wanted someone else to give Him water.

Jesus could erect a church building, but He will not do it without you and me. Jesus could win souls, but He will almost never do it, without you and without me. What does Jesus thirst for today? Souls! Souls! Souls! What will quench the thirst of Jesus? Souls!

Perhaps you are thinking, "Bailey Smith, your imagination is running away with you." Oh, is it? Don't you remember in Matthew 25:35-40 where Jesus told His disciples that they had given Him meat and drink. When they asked Jesus when they had done this, He replied, "Inasmuch as ye have done it unto one of the least of these my brethren, ye have done it unto me." You and I are to help people, care for people, and to bring people to the Cross, that they may know Jesus died for them. Don't you know that the Son of Man came to seek and to save those who are lost! The way you satisfy the thirst of Jesus is reach souls for whom He died!

Have you ever compared the life of Judas with that of John? John is the one who wrote that Jesus said, "I thirst."

I thought of Judas. No one likes Judas. I don't know of anyone who would even name their dog "Judas." We give our children names like John, Mary, or Joshua—but never Judas, that I know of.

Have you compared Judas and John? What did Judas do about the Cross? It hurts me even to talk about Judas, because he is such a bitter illumination of truth. What did Judas do about the Cross? He "made a buck"—thirty pieces of silver! Judas thought to himself, *Jesus is going to die. Jesus is going to suffer and bleed. I believe I can work that out to my financial advantage!* Judas took advantage of Jesus' death in order to line his pockets.

John, on the other hand, gave his all. You and I have a choice to make. We can either use the Cross for our material gain, or we can use it as an opportunity to tell Jesus that we will do our dead-level best.

Today the name of Judas is remembered in disdain and infamy, but the name of John is remembered in loyalty and unselfish, committed discipleship for the Lord Jesus. How are you going to be remembered in decades to come? I hope, as one who did his/her best like John. Don't be like Judas who ignored the Cross and was greedy and selfish, but be a John. Be one who is loving and caring, not one who says, "I'm for old number one. I am interested only in me."

III. A Word of Invitation

As Jesus spoke from the Cross, He gave a word of isolation and a word of identification. He then spoke a sixth word. It was a word of invitation.

Mark what Jesus said in John 19:30 as He was nearing the end of His life. "It is finished!" It is completed. "Tetelestai!" was the Greek rendition of "It is finished!" It literally means, "something has been completed."

There are many forms and uses of that word. However,

its main use involved a prisoner who had his crime paid for. The officials would write the word *tetelestai* upon a piece of parchment which they would nail to the door of the prison. When the guard would come by and see the parchment with the word *tetelestai,* he would take the key and open the door. Then he would tell the prisoner that all of his crimes had been paid for by a friend and that he was free to go.

When Jesus cried, "Tetelestai!" He meant that the entire price of redemption had been paid. There is nothing else you need to do to be saved. You do not need baptism. You do not need the Lord's Supper. Those ordinances are essential to obedience but not to salvation. You do not need good works. You do not need the Book of Mormon. You do not even need a Baptist preacher! It is finished— your sins have been paid for. All of your sins have been cast as far as the East is from the West. They have been placed down into the bottom of the ocean. The ocean at the deepest part is 37,800 feet deep.

Nothing else has to be done. All of the world could be saved by what Jesus did on the Cross. It is finished! All of the debt of sin had been paid. My friend, you can come to God. Your sins can be forgiven. The blood of Christ will wash your sins away, never to be remembered against you. His payment of your sin debt becomes effective when you repent and receive Jesus Christ as your personal Lord and Savior.

The saints of the Old Testament had nothing to worry about. They believed God and on faith accepted the promise of the Redeemer Who was to come. He paid all the demands of prophetic truth, all the demands of the Levitical blood sacrifice, all the demands His Father had upon a substitutionary death. All that God required of you was paid for in the atoning death of Jesus Christ. What a story! "It is finished!"

One of the unusual characteristics of Michelangelo was that he never wanted to finish a work. The Pope had to continually beg him to finish the Sistine Chapel ceiling. Michelangelo left a display called The Sacristy of Michelangelo in Florence, Italy. There you would discover painting after painting and sculpture after sculpture that he started and never finished.

Dr. A. T. Robertson, possibly the greatest Greek scholar in centuries, was translating the New Testament. It was going to be called *The Robertson Translation of the New Testament.* Robertson had been asked to translate the New Testament, being such a Greek scholar, and he was doing so. When he came to Matthew 8, he left his office to go teach his class. He never returned to his earthly home. When they went into Dr. Robertson's office they found his lexicon, his books of cognate languages, all of his papers, and all of his reference books scattered across his desk. There also lay in the handwriting of Dr. Robertson his translation of Matthew 8. He never finished it.

When my father went to look at his new church auditorium in East Dallas, there was nothing but the foundation. In a freak accident, my father was mortally injured and fell, dying upon the foundation of his new Baptist church in East Dallas. My father, the workers reported, kicked a little while and then died right there. I returned to that church several times after that, and I saw that foundation. I said to myself each time, "My Dad's church was unfinished."

Robertson, B. E. Smith, Michelangelo. Maybe your work is unfinished as well. However, Jesus finished it all. Salvation is free, fully paid for. All you must do is accept it.

Tetelestai! It is finished! When they heard that, I believe the birds began to sing, *"Tetelestai!"* The sound of the stream going down the mountains murmured, *"Tetelestai!"* Oh, what Jesus has done for us!

Years ago, I was conducting a revival in Forrest City, Arkansas, a city not far from Memphis. We went one day to a lovely home, built in Georgian architecture. That home was almost totally furnished with antiques. The lady had a beautiful little dog, which was the fattest member of the family. The dog was so well-cared for. It had a rhinestone collar around its neck. It did not even smell like a dog because of the scented powder the lady had put on it.

As we toured her spacious home admiring her antiques, we came to the master bedroom. She had an antique bed with long spires on the bedposts. I looked over into the corner, and there was a little antique bed with spires on the bedposts for the dog.

We sat down to eat. We had roast, potatoes, carrots, and all kinds of luscious food. Over in the corner of the dining room was the dog. The dog ate the same food we did. We had Eagle Brand lemon pie for dessert. The dog had Eagle Brand lemon pie for dessert.

Every place that woman walked around that house, that dog would follow. Finally, I asked, "You have to tell me about your dog." She replied, "Well, I do take care of him. But Preacher, let me tell you why. A few years ago that dog began to bark so ferociously that it awakened me. I didn't know what was going on. It had never barked that way in all of its life. I came into the living room, and there was a man halfway in the window. He had cut the screen and was trying to get in, and the dog was biting him. The dog chased that man out of my house, and he ran across the lawn. Of course, I called the police. I learned the next day that later on that very night, the man raped a woman and murdered her. Had it not been for this dog, I would have been that woman. I know I am silly the way I take care of him, but you have to understand." I answered, "I do."

I don't have any objection to people taking good care of their animals. However, there are many people who give greater care to their dogs than they do to Jesus. You say, "But look at all that dog did for that woman." How about all that Jesus did for you? If a woman can care for a dog that saved her life, can't you care for Jesus Who gave you Eternal Life?

What an opportunity you have to do something for Jesus. Repent of your sin and receive Jesus Christ as your Lord and Savior! Then live for Him in all you do. Do not throw Jesus a bone—give Him your best from every standpoint.

6

The Secret of Ultimate Living

And when Jesus had cried with a loud voice, he said, Father into thy hands I commend my spirit: and having said thus, he gave up the ghost. Now when the centurion saw what was done, he glorified God, saying, Certainly this was a righteous man (Luke 23:46-47).

The last two chapters have examined the words that Jesus spoke from the Cross. As He hung in shame and ignominy on the Roman gibbet, Jesus spoke seven times. He spoke a word of intercession, a word of inspiration, a word of interest, a word of isolation, a word of identification, and a word of invitation.

In this chapter we shall take a further, more in-depth look at our Lord's word of invitation. Then we shall see the secret of ultimate living which is found in Jesus' final word from the Cross as He spoke a word of *invocation*.

John 19:30 records that shortly before He died, Jesus cried out, "It is finished!" This is the English translation of the Greek word "Tetelestai!"

In order to more fully understand the deep meaning contained in this expression, we shall examine this Greek word in minute detail. We are going to deal with the word "Tetelestai" much as a Greek student would in in seminary.

First of all, *Tetelestai* is in the *third person*. Jesus said, "It is finished." He did not say, "I am finished." It is not in the first person, because He was not finished. Rather "it" is finished. The wonderful responsibility He had of completing the redemption of the world had been done.

Second, *Tetelestai* is in the *perfect* tense. Now in Greek the perfect tense denotes action that was begun in the past, continues in the present, and will continue into the future. Thank God, that which began in prophetic truth was completed at Calvary and is continuing today—and shall ever be! The sacrifice never has to be made again. The work of the Cross has never been repeated because it does not need to be. The work of salvation was completed in the past and remains completed in the present and in the future.

Third, *tetelestai* is in the *indicative* mood. This refers to action that is absolutely certain, as opposed to the subjunctive mood which refers to hypothetical action. It is absolutely, incontrovertibly without question that salvation has been paid for on the Cross. That is what *Tetelestai* means. It is literally finished!

Finally, *Tetelestai* is passive *voice*. The passive voice in Greek refers to action that one has done for another. On the Cross, Jesus did all that is necessary for you to make it into Heaven. He did all that is necessary for you to be born again. He did in on behalf of others.

It is finished! Jesus was not finished, salvation was finished! The final word Jesus spoke from the Cross is recorded in Luke 23:46: "Father, into thy hands I commend my Spirit." As soon as Jesus spoke this word of invocation, He gave up His spirit unto His Father, for His redemptive work on earth was completed!

You will notice that Jesus did not do that until He could first of all say, "Tetelestai!" "It is finished!" Salvation had been paid for. Then Jesus gave of Himself totally and completely at the end of His life into the hands of His Father. Contained in those final words is the secret of ultimate living.

Surely it would be a foolish person who would say, "I do not want to live life at its best. I do not want to know the ultimate existence." I am going to share with you how you can live life to such an extent that no one on earth can live better than you. No one can have more than you, if you will listen.

I was reading in a travel magazine where it stated that going to the British Cayman Islands is the ultimate vacation. Going to New Zealand is the ultimate cruise. An airlines magazine claimed Hawaii is the ultimate vacation. I saw on television that to drive a BMW is to drive the ultimate machine. It is no wonder that the Bible declares that Christ came to give life and to give it more abundantly. Only in Jesus will you find life and life to its fullest.

I. The Ultimate Relationship

As we look at the final saying of the Lord Jesus from the Cross, I want you to see, first of all, the ultimate relationship. Jesus said, "Father, . . ." The secret to ultimate living is expressed in an ultimate relationship with the Heavenly Father. Jesus loved that word, "Father."

At the age of twelve, Jesus was in the Temple speaking with the theologians when Mary and Joseph found Him. According to the Scriptures, Jesus asked His mother, "Wist ye not that I must be about my Father's business?" The first recorded words out of the mouth of Jesus indicated that He had a Father in Heaven.

When Jesus preached His Sermon on the Mount, seven-

teen times He mentioned the word "Father." John
records what has been called the "Paschal Discourse."
Forty-five times Jesus uses that word "Father." John 17,
which is known as the "High Priestly Prayer of Jesus,"
contains that word "Father" six more times.

Why is that so? To be able to call God your Father is
life's ultimate relationship. I have been to many seminars
where they tell you how to have a right relationship with
a wife or with a husband. I have been to seminars that tell
you how to have a right relationship with your Mom and
with your Dad or with your children. I have even spoken
in some of those seminars.

However, Jesus is an example of a man who had learned
life's most supreme lesson and that is: Life at its fullest will
have the ultimate relationship. You cannot know ultimate
living unless you have the ultimate relationship. The ultimate relationship is to be able to say, as Jesus did, "Father."

There are two truths about the use of the word "Father" as it relates to you and to me.

A. Limited Knowledge

First of all, we can never know God the Father to the
same extent Jesus did. He is the "only begotten Son of
God." This word "begotten" is a very intimate word. In
fact, it literally means that Jesus was of His Father, God.
He was begotten. As you read the genealogical tables in
the Bible, you will see that so and so begat so and so, who
begat so and so. Generation after generation. These were
the progenitors of those particular people. Jesus literally
was the Son of God!

Now we can become the sons of God but not to the
same extent Jesus was. He was different, special, unique,
distinctive, and one of a kind. We can come to the point
where we can call God our Father. However, we cannot

become the sons of God in the exact way Jesus was and is. He was set apart—one of a kind. We become sons of God through adoption.

B. Limited Humanity

Secondly, only Christians can call God "Father." The Bible does not teach the Fatherhood of God and the brotherhood of man, even though all of us are brothers and sisters to the extent that we all live on planet Earth and therefore have much in common. We walk on the earth and we breath ozygen and we drink water. We are all of Adam's race.

However, one cannot become a child of God and legitimately call God one's Father unless one seeks the Father through His Son, Jesus Christ. Jesus said, "If you have seen Me, you have seen the Father." First, John reminds us that he who neglects the Son has also turned his back upon the Father.

Listen to what Galatians 4:4-7 says, "But when the fulness of the time was come, God sent forth his Son, made of a woman, made under the law, To redeem them that were under the law, that we might receive the adoption of sons. And because ye are sons, God hath sent forth the Spirit of his Son into your hearts, crying, Abba, Father. Wherefore thou art no more a servant, but a son; and if a son, then an heir of God through Christ."

He uses the word "Abba" which is an intimate Aramaic word for "Daddy." It is a personal expression one would use in speaking to one's own father. Those of us who have been saved are allowed to approach God and say, with reverence and respect, "Daddy, my Father, I have a need."

The ultimate relationship of life is to know that you have found God and that you have a relationship with Him as your Heavenly Father. The only way to know God

as your Father is through a salvation experience of knowing Jesus Christ as Savior and Lord. To become a Christian
is to be born again. It is a new birth.

One day I was born physically and became a physical
son of a physical father. Some years after I was born physically, I realized that I was a sinner, that I needed to repent
of my sin and ask Jesus to come into my heart. When I did
so, I not only was a physical son of a physical father, I
became a spiritual son of a spiritual Father.

That is the new birth experience. That is why, if you
want to know life to its ultimate extent, you must have the
ultimate relationship of God in Heaven as your Heavenly
Father. Jesus called from the Cross, "Father."

A little boy had become terribly sick and was dying of
pneumonia. His father leaned over him and said, "Son, I
am so sorry. Are you doing OK? I know you must be
afraid." That boy looked up from his death bed, squarely
into the eyes of his dad, and whispered, "Daddy, if God
is anything like you, then I'm not scared."

Can you cry out to God as your Heavenly Father in your
hour of need, even as Jesus did from the Cross? Do you
know life's ultimate relationship? Can you call Him "Daddy" even as Jesus could? That is the ultimate relationship.

II. The Ultimate Security

Not only does the secret of ultimate living involve the
ultimate relationship, but also it involves the ultimate
security.

The second word Jesus spoke was, "Father, into thy
hands . . ."

A recent Gallup Poll reported that the greatest desire
of most Americans is not money or health—but security.
Sometimes health and wealth will be involved in that
security, to be sure. Yet the number-one comment of

most people who had been interviewed was, "I want to be secure."

I ask you, how can you be any more secure than knowing that you are in the hands of God the Father? To have a "Father," the ultimate relationship; "into Thy hands," the ultimate security.

If there is one facet we remember about our moms and dads, it is their hands. I have heard my wife, Sandy, remark how she often remembers the hands of her mother and how they ministered to her as a little girl.

I remember my mother's hands. If I were an artist, I could take what is in my mind at this moment and draw a perfect picture of my mother's hands. I can see them so well in my mind, just as I can see my father's hands. I remember when I looked into the casket of my father, I saw his hands placed over his chest. I remember noticing that his hands were just like mine—big, rough hands.

My name is "Smith." We come from people who were "blacksmiths" and "silversmiths," people who had to work with their hands. I looked at my father's hands and I thought, *How many times those hands have labored in my behalf. How many times those hands have worked for me.*

Then I looked again and thought, *How many times those hands have gotten my attention!"* They were rough hands and strong arms. Can you imagine how secure we felt?

You remember your mother coming in when you were too sick to go to school. She would hold her hand, feel of your brow, and hope she would feel a very hot head! Then your mother would put her hands on your face. There is nothing like both hands of your mom on your face in love and in compassion.

Jesus told us, not only of the ultimate relationship with the Father, but also of the ultimate security: "Into Thy hands!" To know that you are in the hands of God! How could anyone be more secure than that?

Many things Americans have thought for a long time to be secure are not so secure. We used to think respect for America among our friends around the world was secure, but the Iranian crisis, and other crises, did away with that. We have often thought that we were secure because of our military. Yet when our military went into Iran and our helicopters ran into each other, we learned that not even the American military is invincible.

We thought the American dollar was sound, yet some of the largest banks in the nation have collapsed because of insolvency. We wonder what has happened. Now we read in the *Wall Street Journal* where one farm a day, on the average, is being sold in America because the farmer cannot pay his bills. We are wondering what is happening to the best agricultural system on the face of the earth.

The whole financial system seems to be tottering. The military is not invincible. The respect of our friends is not secure around the world. However, if you have the ultimate relationship to call God your Father and you put your life into His hands, you have the ultimate security. You need never fear anything again.

"Into thy hands!" I love John 10:28, where Jesus asserted, "I give unto them eternal life; and they shall never perish, neither shall any man pluck them out of my hand." The Bible says that when we are saved, God literally has us in the very palm of His hand. Can you imagine the demons of hell, or the devil himself, coming and prying open the hand of God and then, with all of the power of hell, trying to snatch you out of the hand of God? Not on your life! It will never happen!

Once you are born again, once you are saved, as Jesus says in John 10:29, "My Father, which gave them me, is greater than all; and no man is able to pluck them out of my Father's hand." When you are in the hands of God, you are secure. God has you. You can know that once you die you will go immediately into the presence of God.

The very moment you were born again, God built you a mansion up there, and it will never have a "For Sale" sign in front of it. You are secure in the hands of Almighty God. Thank God for that security!

Second Timothy 1:12 says, "I know whom I have believed, and am persuaded that he is able to keep that which I have committed unto him against that day." The word which is translated "know" in this verse is the Greek word *oida*, which literally means "I know *in whom* I have believed. . . ."

If the Greek were to say, "I know whom . . . ," it would be a phrase that would indicate I know God by hearsay. That is, I know God by what others say. However, when you say, "I know *in whom* I believe . . . ," it means I know the inside of the whole story.

I said to a man one time, jokingly, "If I put money in your bank, is it secure?" He became extremely serious and said, "Let me tell you something, I know the inside operations of this bank. I know what we do, and I want to just tell you, because I am an insider, that your money is absolutely secure."

In 2 Timothy 1:12, Paul wrote, "I know *in whom* I have believed." That word "know" literally means to know as an insider. I know as one who has been born again. I know as one who is in the hands of God. I know as one who is secure. I know as one who is satisfied. I know as one who has God in me and I in Him. I know it by experience.

Those of us who have been born again can say, "I know that I am saved forever because it has happened to me. I know in whom I have believed. I am in Christ, and He is in me." Oh, the ultimate security of saying, "Into thy hands."

I do not pace back and forth in front of the bank with a slingshot, wondering if someone is going to steal my money, because I feel it is secure in that particular bank. Even more do I know Whom I believe because I am an insider. I am one of His children. I know that I am secure because of what He has done in my life. That is the ultimate security.

To be in the hands of God is not always good! Hebrews 10:31 says, "It is a fearful thing to fall into the hands of a living God." If you have never been born again—one day you will fall into the hands of God; unredeemed, unsaved, unconverted, not a Christian. Do not let your lost life fall into the hands of God, but give your life to Jesus and have the ultimate security.

The hands of God scooped up the valleys. The hands of God heaped up the mountains. The hands of God flung the luminaries into space. The hands of God started the comets around the solar system. The hands of God created you and me. God's hands!

I was reading the other day the statistics of how massive this universe is. If you were to travel at the speed of light, 186,282 miles per second, in two seconds you would pass the moon. In eight minutes you would pass the sun. In five months you would be at the edge of the solar system. In four and one-half years you would arrive at our nearest star, Alpha Centauri.

If you were to travel one million five hundred thousand years at 186,282 miles per second, you would arrive at our nearest galactic neighbors, the Magellanic Clouds. Those are just the closest galaxies to the Milky Way. Yet there are untold millions of galaxies in the universe!

If you were to travel for a billion years or a trillion years at 186,282 miles per second, you would never come to the end of God's universe! Yet I read from Isaiah 40:12 that God has all of the oceans right in the hollow of His hand.

God's hand is so big that you could put every body of water into the hollow of His hand.

The next phrase in the King James Version does not do it justice. The King James Version says, "meted out heaven with the span." When I was in Atlanta, Charles Stanley gave me a *New International Version* of the Bible. The *New International Version* translates Isaiah 40:12 thusly, "Who had measured the waters in the hollow of His hand, or with the breadth of His hand marked off the heavens."

God says that when He measured the heavens, He measured them by the breadth of His hand. All of the heavens I have mentioned are not as big as God's hand is wide. He has measured the heavens by the breadth of His hand, and He has measured out the waters of the world in the hollow of His hand.

Can you imagine, not only the ultimate relationship with the Father, but also the ultimate security of being in hands like the hands of Almighty God!

III. The Ultimate Commitment

Not only is ultimate living composed of the ultimate relationship and the ultimate security, but there is also the ultimate commitment. Jesus said, "Father, into Thy hands, I commend. . . ." The word "commend" is the Greek Word "paratithemai." It means "to deposit a thing, to place a thing to one's charge or to one's trust." Jesus literally said, "Father, I totally commit Myself unto You."

This Greek word also means "to deliver." When Jesus said "I commend," He meant, "I deliver My life unto Your hands." In John 10 when they tried to crucify Jesus, Jesus said to Herod Antipas, "No man takes my life from me." Jesus was not caught in a criminal act and did not die as a martyr. Jesus' death was planned from before the beginning of time. No one grabbed Jesus and threw Him on a

Roman cross. He willingly died, and the plan and the prophecy of God's act of redemption were completed.

When Pontius Pilate became arrogant with Jesus while He stood before him, Jesus said a most interesting thing. "Pilate, you have no power that my Father in heaven does not give to you. You cannot sentence Me to die unless it is the will of My Father. You cannot take My life from Me." When Jesus said, "I commend . . . ," He was really saying, "God, I literally take My life and deliver it unto You. I give it unto You."

I am not impressed with the people who say, "I just manage my own life, Preacher. I live my own life." Those men do not astound me or impress me. They certainly do not impress God with "I am the master of my own fate. I pull myself up by my own boot straps. Preacher, I want you to know that I am a self-made man!"

That word *paratithemai* literally means "to deliver one's soul," "to deliver one's life by one's own choice, by one's own volition."

God will not force heaven upon you. God will not force love upon you. God will not force His grace. The ultimate commitment is to give your life, to deliver your life, your soul into the hands of God. That is the smartest decision you will ever make.

A girl was at a famous lodge. As she was sitting in a chair, a man noticed she was fanning herself with a silk fan. The man asked, "Little girl, may I borrow that fan overnight?" "No Sir!" she cried and ran off. The parents learned that the man who wanted to borrow that fan was a famous artist. What he wanted to do was to take that silk fan and paint a beautiful picture on it. The fan then would have been worth from $2,500 to $10,000. But the girl said "no!" How many times God has wanted to pick up your life, but He would not grab it. He wanted you to *paratithemai*—to deliver it, to trust it to Him.

That is the ultimate commitment. When you deliver your all to God, He takes it and makes a beautiful picture out of your life. No matter what you have done, no matter how low you have lived, no matter how evilly you have let the years consume your life, I promise you on the authority of God's Word that He will accept your life today.

He will change it from the plain life it is today, and by the time He is through with it, you will be more valuable than you ever have been. Let God have your life.

I read about a man who was a drunken slave trader whose words of profanity shocked even the evil people around him—a man who had nothing on his mind but being a womanizer, drinking liquor, stealing slaves and then selling them for large profits. That man became converted. His name was John Newton. He would write "Amazing Grace, how sweet the sound, That saved a wretch like me. I once was lost, but now am found, Was blind, but now I see."

If God can take a drunken slave trader and make him the writer of such a song, I have an idea that if you will commit your life to God, He can do something with you.

A man alibied to me not long ago, "Preacher, if I could have a 'Saul of Tarsus conversion,' I would be converted too." I inquired, "What do you mean?" He went on, "If I could see a brilliant light from Heaven . . ."

Do you realize what Saul said after that? "I was not disobedient to the heavenly vision." It was not the blinding light that saved him—it was his reaction to it.

Many brilliant lights testify today that Christ is the answer. The real church does. The Word of God does. The changed lives of men like Charles Colson, John Newton, and thousands of other people do.

Christian, you are a brilliant light that testifies to the fact that one day you were lost, undone, and unworthy.

Then, all of a sudden, because you chose the ultimate relationship of letting God be your Father, you had the ultimate security of putting your life into His hands. Through that experience you have become God's child. Your life has been transformed.

There are lights all over this world that shout, "Jesus is the answer!" If you want a brilliant light, look around you. There are many who have been changed by the living Christ.

IV. The Ultimate Success

There is the ultimate relationship, the ultimate security, and the ultimate commitment. Finally, there is the ultimate success.

Jesus cried, "Father, into Thy hands I commend My spirit." He is body, soul, and spirit. The soul is your mind, will, and emotion. When you die, you leave your body and soul, and your spirit goes somewhere. It either goes to be with God in Heaven, or it goes to everlasting death with Satan in eternal judgment and in hell.

Jesus said, "I commit unto you My spirit." That is the ultimate success. I promise you there is one reality in the future of everyone, outside of the return of Christ, and that is death!

Have you ever noticed how everyone else is getting older except you and me? Several months ago a couple came to visit us. They had graduated with Sandy and me from our college in Arkansas. I looked at that man, and I thought to myself, *Man, that guy sure has aged.* Sandy and I later got in the car and drove off. We were talking about the man's wife when Sandy inquired, "Did you see her?" Bailey, I don't look as old as she does, do I?" What do you think I said? I am still healthy! Of course, I said, "No, Honey, you don't."

For years I have had people remark, "You know, Brother Bailey, I went to a reunion of my graduating class, and you cannot believe how some of those people looked!" What they are saying is, "I cannot believe how old so and so looked." (You know, some hair turns grey; some turns loose!) We always think that someone else is getting old— but not us.

One man came back from the doctor. He looked to be in such despair that his friends asked, "What's wrong? Why are you so discouraged?"

"I went to the doctor. Now I have to take a pill a day for the rest of my life."

"Man, that's no problem. A lot of people take a pill a day."

"Yes, but he gave me only four pills!"

My dad used to comment, "Son, you get to high school, and that will be an obstacle. You will get to college, and that will be an obstacle. You will get to seminary, and that will be an obstacle. Now, one of two things is going to happen. Either high school will defeat you, and you will drop out, or college will defeat you, and you will drop out, or seminary will defeat you, and you will drop out. Or else, you will defeat them. What are you going to do?"

When I went to high school, I recalled that my dad said high school could stop me, and I might drop out, so I was not going to be defeated. So I went on. The same with college and graduate school.

I have a choice and you have a choice. One day I am going to face death. I can either be defeated by death or I can defeat it. I am not going to allow death to defeat me, because I am in Christ who is in God. I am in God's hands.

Christ has already gone through the grave and knocked the end out of it. He reached down and pulled the stinger out of death. Now death has no victory. There is now no sting in the grave because of what Jesus has done on the Cross. I will not be defeated by death, because death, through Christ, has already been defeated! Why should I march headlong into my future and be defeated by that which has already been defeated?

How foolish it would be for a man to skimp and save all of his life, never take a vacation, never eat out, and enjoy himself—then come to be seventy years of age, retire, get out of his business, and then take all the money he has saved to the river and throw it in. What a foolish man! No more foolish than some of you who would live all of your life without Jesus and then throw it into an everlasting hell.

My friend, God loves you so much. You can have life to its ultimate. "Father"—the ultimate relationship! "Into Thy hands"—the ultimate security! "I commend"—the ultimate commitment! Then the ultimate success when you can face death, and it does not bother you a bit.

I love being a Christian because we can face death even with a sense of humor. One friend of mine had his preacher father look up at him and say, "Son, I want you to preach my funeral, and if you will do it, I will never ask you to do it again."

I stood around the bedside of a woman who had lived such a godly life. She had six sons around her. Her long grey hair that had not been cut since she was a girl was lying upon that pillow. That woman was near death, and she began to sing that song we used to sing in the country, "This world is not my home, I'm just a-passing through, my treasures are laid up somewhere beyond the blue."

Then she looked at one of her sons and said, "Ted, I want you to thank Jesus that your mother is about to die." "But Mother . . . !" "Ted, I want you to thank Jesus that I am about to go home to be with Him."

That young boy, with a broken voice, could hardly pray and he began, "God, I thank you for Mother. I thank you for my Christian home. I thank You for what she has taught me. I thank You that I learned the Bible at her knee. I thank you that she was an example of godliness." He did not want to pray it, but he did, "God, I thank you that Mother is about to leave us to go to be with you."

When they opened their eyes their mother's quiet form was lying upon that bed. The boys turned to one another, and they said, "Well, Mother taught us how to live. Men, just now she taught us how to die."

The ultimate success is when you come to the end of this life, and there is Jesus waiting to receive you.

7

What a Difference Easter Makes

And it came to pass, as he sat at meat with them, he took bread, and blessed it, and brake it, and gave to them. And their eyes were opened, and they knew him: and he vanished out of their sight. And they said one to another, Did not our heart burn within us, while he talked with us by the way, and while he opened to us the scriptures? And they rose up the same hour, and returned to Jerusalem, and found the eleven gathered together, and them that were with them. Saying, The Lord is risen indeed, and hath appeared to Simon. And they told what things were done in the way, and how he was known of them in breaking of bread. And ye are witnesses of these things. And, behold, I send the promise of my Father upon you; but tarry ye in the city of Jerusalem, until ye be endued with power from on high. And he led them out as far as to Bethany, and he lifted up his hands, and blessed them. And it came to pass, while he blessed them, he was parted from them, and carried up into heaven. And they worshipped him, and returned to Jerusalem with great joy; And were continually in the temple, praising and blessing God. Amen (Luke 24:30-35, 48-53).

In 1957 a song entitled "What a Difference a Day Makes" sold more than two million copies. When I ponder that song, I realize that could apply to many dates in our history. "December 7, 1941." You would immediately know the difference that day made in history.

I talked with the man who first spotted those Japanese planes coming toward Pearl Harbor. His name was Peterson, and he sounded the alarm, warning the Americans of what was taking place. What a difference that particular day made in history.

August 6, 1945, was another day that made a difference. On that date, for the first time in history, an atomic bomb was dropped on mankind, on the city of Hiroshima. Three days later, on August 9, another atomic bomb was dropped on Nagasaki. What a difference those days made.

We could talk about a day in 1492, resulting in the discovery of the New World. What a difference that day made. The day you were born certainly was one where a difference was made.

How about the day of the birth of Jesus Christ? What a difference that day has made to a watching world. The day our Lord Jesus Christ was born.

However, the greatest day in history was the day that Jesus Christ was resurrected from the grave! That glorious Resurrection Day in AD 30 was the first Easter Sunday!

Those of us who are saved understand that the reason we come to church on Sunday is because Sunday is the Son's Day—the day of His resurrection (see Acts 20:7). No longer is the Sabbath our primary day of worship. Ever since Jesus burst forth out of the grave, having conquered death and hell, Christians have worshiped on Sunday— the first day of the week. In so doing, we celebrate the "Lord's Day"—the day of His resurrection.

I want to ask you a question of a practical nature: What difference does Easter make? Who cares? Do you care? Has it made any difference in your life?

What a difference a day makes, that day of the resurrection of Jesus Christ. When you really see the difference

Easter made in the New Testament, you will see what a glorious difference it can make in your life, in the life of the church, in the life of our denomination, and in the life of this country. I want to share five ideas about where Easter should make a difference.

I. A Difference in Endurance

First of all, Easter should make a difference in our endurance. Those New Testament disciples felt as if death had conquered their cause and there was no hope. There was nothing but dejection, despair, and discouragement —because they believed God had died.

For Jesus, the Son of God and God in the flesh, to die was for God Himself to die. They could not imagine that. The farthest thought from their minds was that God Himself would die upon a cruel Roman cross. You can imagine the despair. Then the morning came that Jesus burst forth from that grave.

The lesson God wants us to learn is this: There is never a time in the life of a Christian when he should despair. When the Cross of Christ came, there was nothing but dejection and discouragement. Almost all of the disciples left Him because they thought the cause was over. They thought Jesus was done in once and for all. Every apostle except the Apostle John abandoned Jesus and hid in fear, according to the Bible.

I want to paint for you the most obvious picture of despair and discouragement you could possibly view. Even in such a moment, God came through. The light came through the darkness. The crucifixion turned to resurrection. Death turned to life. Darkness turned to light. Remember: God's delays are not God's denials, and God's detours are not God's desertions. God may delay you, but He will not deny you. God may detour you, but He will not desert you.

God not only acts according to your needs, He also acts according to the best timing. There is no place for you to despair, no place for you to lament, "Man, things are turning against me! What am I going to do?"

Sir Winston Churchill was invited to deliver the commencement address at Harvard one year. As he rose to speak, he looked out across the graduating class and said, "Never, never, never give up!" Then he sat down.

There is no place for you to give up. Some of you have certain areas, circumstances, and encounters of your life you cannot conquer. You think that somehow you must quit. The resurrection of Jesus Christ tells you that no matter how dark it is, you do not have to give up. When your ideas, dreams, and plans meet a dead-end street, when your hopes seem to die—not even then is the time to give up.

From the moment in history when God in the flesh died there emerged resurrection. There came power and there came light. There came life and there came future. No matter how dark circumstances seem to be, there is never a time in the life of a child of God when he ought to conclude, "That's it! I quit! I throw in the towel! I give up!" If God can reach down and bring a dead man to life, He can handle your situation.

When Jesus came into Bethany, He was met by Mary and Martha, the sisters of Lazarus. What they said to Jesus was most revealing. "Master, had you been here our brother would not have died." I think they were really saying to Jesus, "Lord, you flat blew it! Lord, you have goofed up. Jesus, it is all your fault that our brother is dead! Had you come on time Lazarus would not have died."

I have a word for you. Jesus has never been late. You say, "Boy, He makes you sweat, though." He sure does! You will come to the point where you think God is late and that God is not going to come through.

The reason Jesus delayed His coming to Bethany is that He wanted Lazarus to die Why? It is a greater miracle to raise a man from the dead than it is to keep a man from dying. Jesus knew that if He showed up they would expect healing, but He did not want healing. He wanted resurrection.

Some of us have cried, stomped, and had a nervous breakdown, wondering why God has not given us what we wanted. The reason is we do not know what is best for us. God may withhold something you want in order to give you something you did not know was available.

"Jesus, had you just done it the way I wanted it. Had you just helped me, had you just strengthened me, had you just been there in that circumstance, then I would not be in this mess in the first place." Yet, through the so-called mess you are in, God is going to make a greater victory than if He had prevented the circumstance in the first place. Thus, the resurrection of Jesus Christ ought to make a difference in your endurance! No matter what situation you are in, no matter how badly your back is against the wall, you can endure. The resurrection declares that when the worse point in history came, the death of Jesus, God was still not through—and He is not through with you, either.

Picture in your mind David's encounter with Goliath. Can you imagine what must have gone on before that? The Philistines were lined up across the valley from the Israelites. Goliath was in their midst taunting the Israelites. Time and again those Israelites prayed for God to intervene. I would imagine you, too, have prayed to God to act in reference to the giant problems of your life. All of us have faced a Goliath, and we have asked God to move against him.

The Israelites were lined up on one side of the valley. Goliath and the Philistines were on the opposite side. The

Israelites were so fearful that their knees were smiting one against another. I am certain they must have prayed like this: "God, across the battlefield there is a giant. God, do you see him over there? Lord, he is a whopper. That is the biggest creature I have ever seen. Now, God, I tell you what I want." (See if this isn't a Baptist prayer.) "God, I am going to pray and when I count three, I want to see a dead giant. Now here we go. God, You just revealed to me that this is what you are going to do. 'Dear God, take care of that giant, whip him, knock him down, clobber him in the head, put him flat of his back in the name of the God of Israel. I know you are going to do it.'

"God, he is still there! Knock him down! Maybe You did not hear. I am going to try one more time: 'God, there is a big giant, and I am scared of him. God, you told me You would not put more on me than I can bear, and I cannot bear that giant and, God, I pray right now that you will just do something dramatic! God, if you do, I will give you the glory. God, I want you to strike that giant with a bolt of lightning right now.'"

Then, all of a sudden there came a little shepherd boy with a slingshot. Do you believe any Israelite bowed his head and prayed, "God, there is a big giant. Would you bring a twelve-year-old boy to kill him?" David did not seem to be an answer to prayer. David was God's means of doing what needed to be done. Most of the time when you ask for God to act He will not do so the way you think He will.

You may become so frustrated and so upset because you prayed for this or that, yet God has not come through dramatically or spiritually as you had anticipated.

Do not try to judge God by your experiences or by those of someone else. Put your faith in the living God and trust His Word. God is going to answer your prayers. You can make it. God's answer may not be what you expected, but

God will answer. Easter ought to make a difference in your endurance.

Daniel perhaps thought those lions would eat him up, but they did not. He endured. Perhaps the three Hebrew children thought the fiery furnace would incinerate them, but it did not. They endured. Perhaps Jonah thought that when that great fish swallowed him, that was the end of it. It was not, for God brought a mighty victory from it. *You* can endure. The resurrection is an illustration of that.

II. A Difference in Enthusiasm

Not only should Easter make a difference in your endurance, it ought to do the same in your enthusiasm. After Jesus appeared to two of His followers on the Road to Emmaus, they testified, "Did not our heart burn within us while He talked with us by the way?" Luke 14:52 notes, "And they worshipped Him . . . with great joy." The following verse states that they "were continually in the temple, praising and blessing God."

When you understand what the resurrection means, you will not have to work up excitement. You will be excited! You will not have to work up enthusiasm. It will be as natural as day following night. It is actually the supernatural result of what God is about.

Sometime ago, I was in the Atlanta airport, and I was walking behind some men who looked like businessmen. They had all the trappings: three-piece suits with four buttons on each sleeve, starched white shirts with silk ties, and brief cases. I followed them right into the men's room. There they put down their brief cases, got into a huddle, and said, "Yea!" I thought to myself, *What a place to celebrate!* So I stood there listening for a moment. It seems they had come from an airport restaurant where they had sealed a deal and made a $30,000 commission.

They were celebrating. You have never seen such excitement in your life.

I thought to myself, *You know, I ought to be happy all the time because I have the living Lord in my heart. I have a reason to be enthusiastic. I have a reason to rejoice. I am well aware of the scripture that Jesus is alive and real! He has never been more alive than He is right now.* What a difference it makes in our enthusiasm!

Here was a dejected, discouraged apostle named Peter. He was found warming himself by the enemies' fire, found cursing and denying his Lord. Then in a short time he became an eloquent, powerful preacher on the Day of Pentecost. What made the difference? How did Simon Peter turn from a coward to a crusader? It happened when Peter knew that Jesus was alive! The resurrection!

How did those early disciples who could not stand the crucifixion suddenly become powerful missionaries and spread Christianity across the earth like a prairie fire? What made the difference? They knew the One who went into the tomb had come out victoriously.

Easter can make a difference in your enthusiasm for life. Christmas has no meaning without the resurrection. Thanksgiving is a hoax without the resurrection. Your own birth is nothing but an entrance into a gloomy, dark, dead-end street, had it not been for the resurrection of Jesus Christ.

A policeman in Chicago came upon a man who was kneeling on a sidewalk. The man got up, put his hands up towards a building, and talked out loud, moving his lips rather rapidly. The policeman later reported that he thought the man was a lunatic or a drunk. The policeman came over and asked, "Sir, what are you doing?" When the man turned around the policeman recognized him to be the famous evangelist, Billy Sunday. Billy Sunday explained, "Oh, Officer, I know I am acting strange, but this little building here is where I got saved. Once a year I come back and just thank God for meeting me here." "Mr. Sunday," the officer answered, "you go ahead and pray all you want to; I will keep the crowd away."

When the disciples were filled with the Spirit on the Day of Pentecost, people thought they were drunk. They were right! The disciples were drunk but not with wine. They were drunk with the Holy Ghost! They were full of God, full of the Spirit. Sometimes when we become so full of God we have such an enthusiasm that the world does not understand.

When I consider the conquering Christ of Calvary coming forth out of that grave, I cannot help but be bubbly and effervescent and joyful. I have no room in my life for despair, for Christ is so real. Christ is so powerful and so alive I must be excited about His glorious work!

III. A Difference in Evangelism

Not only does Easter make a difference in endurance and in enthusiasm, it also makes a difference in evangelism. If I had to tell people that Jesus was an ethical, moral leader who taught many ideas for three years, and then died a premature death at thirty-three, leaving us only a good example about how to live, I would not have a unique message.

The Koran contains some teachings similar to those of Jesus. They almost seem parallel at times, but there is a vast difference. Mohammed died and he is still dead. Buddha died and he is still dead. Stalin died and he is still dead. Karl Marx died and he is still dead.

Jesus died and He lives! Oh, what a difference!

There are two considerations regarding evangelism as it relates to the resurrection. First of all, in Acts 17:31 God says that the world will be judged by Jesus Christ whom

He has raised from the dead. In other words, if you reject Christ, you will one day stand before the Son of God.

Buddha will have to stand before Jesus. Mohammed will have to stand before Jesus. Reverend Moon will have to stand before the Son and give account for how he used his life. All of us will. So the resurrection shows that Jesus Christ will be the Judge before whom people will stand.

Second, Acts 10 says, speaking about Jesus, "and he shall judge the quick and the dead." Indeed He will. Jesus shall sit in judgment over us all.

Recently, my friend Cal Chappell invited me to attend a Gideon breakfast. The guest speaker said that in France there are 75,000 cities and towns that have no Christian witness. One out of twelve persons in Paris, France, has never held a Bible in their hand.

Had the early New Testament Christians won their world to Christ, they would have won a number of people equal to the present population of the United States of America. Today America's population represents only 7 percent of the total population of the earth. Yet in the United States are 91 percent of all Christian ministries. That means 9 percent of the Christian witnesses are trying to minister to 93 percent of the world. We live in a world that gravely needs an evangelistic voice.

At Del City for the closing night of our revival, we rented the Fairgrounds Arena. More than seven hundred people came to know Christ as Lord and Savior during the week. Of the five thousand who were present on that Friday night, close to five hundred gave their lives to Christ when the invitation was presented.

As I looked at those brown, black, white, red, and yellow faces of the people who came down, I realized that we are doing a sorry job of reaching this world for Christ. Jesus died so men can live, regardless of the color of their skins. We must be concerned about people coming to know Christ as Lord and Savior and being filled with the Holy Spirit. The resurrection of Jesus Christ makes a difference in my evangelism. I am convinced that people can be saved.

A sweet lady called me early last week and she said, "Brother Bailey, I have called three pastors and asked them to go visit my Dad who is not a Christian. They always say, 'Well, I will send an associate,' but they have not even done that. My dad watches you on television, so would you personally go?" I replied, "Certainly, I will go."

I went to the man's home and was greeted by him and his sweet wife. I would guess he was about sixty-five years of age. I sat down and we small talked for a while. Finally, I explained to him the plan of salvation—how Jesus died upon the Cross and how He rose from the grave. I asked him, "Sir, would you like to receive Christ as Savior?" I stretched my hand as far as I could, and I said, "Would you just put your hand in mine, and would you pray and invite Jesus in?" That older man put his hand in mine and prayed to invite Jesus Christ into his heart. What a glorious, hallelujah experience that was.

The world has not rejected Jesus; we have kept Him a secret! We must be telling, we must be sharing, we must be giving the good news of Christ! When I realize that Christ Jesus came forth out of that grave, I am aware that one day He is coming back. I also realize that the Holy Spirit of God can live within my heart. We must tell somebody! The world is lost and Jesus is coming. It is time to quit playing our little church games and start telling this world that Jesus can change its life.

I care not what has happened in your past, what sins have pulled you down—you can have victory. Kick the cocaine. Pour out the whisky. Quit your wife-swapping and turn your life over to Jesus, because if you are full of Jesus you will not need garbage! There is a new wonderfully full life in Christ. Give your life to Him. What a difference Easter makes in evangelism.

IV. A Difference in Everyday Living

Not only does Easter make a difference in our endurance, in our enthusiasm, and in our evangelism, but it counts in our everyday living.

The late Vance Havner was right when he opined that when a Christian really becomes normal, most other Christians are so subnormal they think that is abnormal. Watchman Nee, the famous devotional author, wrote that *"The Normal Christian Life* is a day of prayer, Bible reading, soul-winning, and design for God to be in full control of one's life. If you are not normally daily in prayer, in Bible reading, in being busy for your church, in witnessing, then you are not the Christian God expects you to be.

A "normal Christian" is not casual. A normal Christian life is characterized by saying, "Speak, Lord, for thy servant heareth," and then acting upon what He says. Anointed and filled with the Holy Spirit, your life is in the control of God. That is the normal Christian life.

We come into that understanding by knowing the power of the resurrection of Christ. Consider what Paul wrote in Philippians 3:10, "That I may know Him, and the power of His resurrection!" There is power for daily living in the resurrection of Jesus Christ. The normal daily existence for a Christian is staying in the Word, sharing your faith, and living every day in the power of the Spirit.

What is a person like when he is right with God? This is my own definition: a person who is right with God is one who could learn on Sunday that he is going to die on Tuesday and yet would do nothing different on Monday.

A lady caught Martin Luther in his garden and inquired, "Mr. Luther, what would you do if you knew you were going to die at midnight tonight?" He replied,

"Madam, the first thing I would do is finish hoeing my garden." That is a good answer. If you would have to change your living because you discovered that you had only two days to live, then you had better change it anyway! A Christian ought always to live with a suitcase packed. I am talking about your "glory suitcase." You ought to live in a normal, everyday existence—full of God.

Have you ever caused a preacher any concern? Has a preacher ever had reason to ponder these questions about you: *I wonder why he is not here more often? I wonder if that person really has a daily Bible reading? I wonder if he/she is really winning souls?*

The normal Christian existence ought to be total faithfulness to God and to the church, daily in His Word, in prayer, and to the work of the church. Can you imagine what would happen if we would let resurrection power be our normal daily experience? What a difference it would make.

V. A Difference in Enemies

Finally, Easter ought to make a difference in our enemies. The Bible indicates we have three enemies: the world, the flesh, and the devil. What does the resurrection do about our enemies? The Bible says in 1 John 2:15, "Love not the world, neither the things that are in the world. If any man love the world, the love of the Father is not in him." Because of the resurrection, we are one day going to leave this world for an infinitely better one.

A little girl in a horrible rainstorm in Chicago looked up and saw the skies green and black. She burst through the door of Dwight L. Moody's office and cried to him, "Mr. Moody, Mr. Moody, the world is coming to an end!" He said, "That's all right, Honey, we can live without it!" We can indeed! We are going to leave this old world.

A second enemy is the flesh. I have had people quip,

"Well, Preacher, I guess the devil did it." Do you realize that if the devil were to die, you would still sin? Matthew declares that out of the heart comes forth lying and thievery and murder and adultery. The devil is not your problem—it is your filthy heart. People question, "Why doesn't God kill the devil?" That is not your biggest problem. Your heart is.

Not only do we face the world and the flesh but also the devil. It is not just temptation that bothers us—it is the Tempter himself. When Jesus came forth from the grave, He defeated the devil. Satan has been conquered. He is a defeated enemy, and he knows it. Yet he still tries to make temporary gains and win fleeting victories. However, one day he is going to be chained and thrown into the pit.

The Bible teaches that the devil is the accuser of the brethren. The next time the devil accuses you of your past sins, you come back with, "Jesus died on the Cross and was resurrected from the dead. Because of that you have no right to accuse me of those sins. They have been washed away by the blood of the Cross. Jesus Christ lives within my heart, and I have the victory over you. Devil, you do whatever you want to, but I am going to leave this old world!"

There is a difference when you understand the resurrection power in your life as you confront your enemies. Temptation has never changed. It is still the same as recorded in 1 John 2:16—"the lust of the flesh, and the lust of the eyes, and the pride of life."

What a difference Easter can make in endurance, in enthusiasm, in evangelism, in everyday living, and in dealing with one's enemies!

8

The Man Who Wore
the First Jesus Shirt

And they crucified him, and parted his garments, casting lots:
that it might be fulfilled which was spoken by the prophet. They
parted my garments among them, and upon my vesture did they
cast lots (Matthew 27:35).

Imagine, if you will, that it is Saturday night. There is
a gala party with festivities. The dogs are barking on the
outside as the chariots are rumbling on the busy streets.

There is tremendous excitement in Jerusalem because
the city has just experienced an eventful moment. The
day before a rebellious "trouble maker" from Nazareth
had been killed. Now they are celebrating because he is
dead. They are excited that the Roman government and
the religious leaders have been victorious.

Suddenly, a golden chariot pulled by three magnificent
horses arrives. From that chariot steps a beautiful woman
with her Roman escort. The two of them walk into a home
where the party is at its loudest peak.

Then they notice that he is dressed like no one else at
the party. They comment with wonderment, "What do
you have on? We have never seen such a gorgeous robe.

Why, it is even seamless!" The man pulls back his shoulders and, with a rather flippant attitude, boasts, "Why, this is my Jesus garment!"

"Your Jesus garment? Do you mean Jesus as in the name of the man we killed yesterday?"

The Roman soldier said, "Yeah, that's right! This is my Jesus garment. Do you remember when a few of us were casting lots at the foot of the Cross? Do you remember that while He died alone with those thieves, I was the guy who won the robe. I call this my Jesus shirt."

When I was in high school, you would never have thought of having a T-shirt or a sweat shirt with the name of Jesus on it. It would have seemed disrespectful. However, since the "Jesus revolution," we have all kinds of slogans such as: "When the rapture occurs, this shirt is going to be left behind." I saw on a T-shirt not long ago, written in the script of Coca-cola, "Jesus is the real thing." One little boy wore a shirt which read, "I'm a little Jesus freak."

You can find Jesus bumper stickers, Jesus shirts, and even Jesus pins. Every Christian book store has so many articles with the name of Jesus on them, which we would not have seen twenty years ago.

However, like the Roman soldier who had a Jesus shirt, yet did not know who Jesus was, you too can have Jesus on your key chains, Jesus on your shirts, Jesus on your bumper stickers, Jesus on your signs, and Jesus all around you—and not have Jesus in your heart.

The Roman soldier who won our Lord's robe missed the whole message of the person, life, and ministry of the Lord Jesus. As I read the story of the crucifixion of Christ, and about the Roman soldier who gambled for the robe of Jesus, I notice that this Roman soldier made four obvious mistakes.

I. He Chose a Secondhand Robe

The Roman soldier received what belonged to Christ but never actually received Christ, as far as we know. He chose a secondhand robe, rather than a firsthand relationship with the Savior. It is possible for you to have what belongs to Christ without belonging to Him.

What are some of the things belonging to Jesus? The educational systems across this country rightfully belong to Christ. They belong to His life and to His influence. The oldest educational institution in America is Harvard University. Harvard began when a preacher put in his will that his theological library would be left to a group of people who wanted to train preachers to preach the gospel of Christ.

A Presbyterian preacher started Princeton University. He met in a log cabin on a river in Buck County, Pennsylvania, and decided that would be the place and the time to start a university to train men as Presbyterian ministers.

On the Continent, Oxford and Cambridge were begun by two preachers who decided that men who preached the gospel needed to be educated so they might not be an embarrassment to the gospel.

Yale University was started by two men who believed that the most important truth in the world is that Jesus Christ was and is the only Son of God.

Go from the institutions of higher education to the public school system that was started by a great theologian, John Calvin. Calvin injected into public education the precepts and approaches that carry over until today.

The influence of Christ has been amazing in the area of education. The educational institutions of today owe their beginnings to the concepts and teachings of the Lord Jesus Christ.

It is no different in art, literature, and music. When you talk about the greatest music, you think of Handel, Mendelssohn, and Bach. If you were to remove the influence of Christ from classical music, that music would not be worth hearing.

What about art? Look at the works of Raphael and Michelangelo. What about literature? Extract Jesus from Milton or Spenser or Shakespeare or Dante, and you will find little left to read.

Consider sculpture. Take away the influence of Jesus from Michelangelo and from Thor Walsden, and you do not have much left. The influence of Christ is in art, in music, and in literature. These are all the robes of Jesus. These are the garments that have shrouded the person and life of Jesus Christ for century upon century.

What is another possession of Christ? The Bible. It is "The Jesus Book." From the beginning of Genesis to the end of Revelation it is the story of Christ, the Son of the Living God.

The Bible is the infallible, inerrant Word of God. That means the Bible is infallible in its truth, that you can find nothing expressed in the Bible that is not absolutely, totally true. When I declare that the Bible is inerrant, I mean that when it speaks regarding history or science or theology, the Bible in every regard is absolutely correct, without error and without contradiction.

I also believe in the plenary verbal inspiration of the Bible. Plenary means complete in all aspects. That is, the Bible is completely inspired—all of it! Verbal means that every word of the Bible is inspired by God.

Obviously I do not enjoy reading the Book of Numbers as much as I do reading the Book of John, but the Book of Numbers is fully as inspired as the Book of John. You might find it difficult to read the Book of Ezekiel or embarrassing to read the Song of Solomon or inspiring to read the Book of Psalms, but they are all equally inspired by God.

Consider the church? I love the institution called the church. Jesus bought it with his blood. It is His Bride. God has chosen His church to carry the glorious gospel.

What about the hymns we sing? When we sing, "It Is Well with My Soul," I am blessed. When I sing, "I Shall Behold Him," and the other songs by Fanny Crosby, I am blessed. I become excited when we sing the hymns of faith. Those are the possessions, those are the garments, those are the robes of Jesus Christ.

However, it is possible for you to love the Imperials and love the Cathedrals and love the Happy Goodman Family —and not know Jesus. It is possible for you to enjoy going to church and possible for you to enjoy the Scriptures and possible for you to appreciate Christian art and Christian literature and Christian music, and yet have absolutely no knowledge of who Jesus Christ really is.

The Roman soldier had the outer garment of Christ, but he never had the inner experience of Christ. He had what belonged to Jesus, but he himself never belonged to Him. Am I talking to you today? You enjoy the fellowship of the church; the good music, the art, and the literature. You appreciate the fact that Christians started the first hospitals in Rome and Constantinople. You realize it was Wesley and Whitefield, preaching in the South, who started the first orphanages in America. Yet, all of those are nothing more than the robes of Christ, the garments of Christ, the matters that belong to Jesus Christ.

Could it be that you appreciate—even love and adore and take part in—the belongings of Christ, but you yourself do not belong to Him? This is the tragedy I see all across this country.

God wants you to be born again. He wants you to be transformed. He wants you to have that exchange of natures. He does not merely want you to accumulate Christian art, activity, Christian possessions, and church business. He wants you to have an inner life that every moment of every day is possessed by Him. As you walk and breathe, He wants you to be obedient to the Word of God and to love Him with all of your heart.

Christian, one day you saw that you were lost and undone and needed to be born again. From the moment of your salvation, your life has been changed, and you are the possession of the Lord Christ.

There are people all over this world who go to a bland, benign worship service where no gospel is preached, no gospel is sung, no heart is changed, no home is transformed, no vows are renewed, no commitments are made, and people go out as lifeless as when they entered. They hear a lecture on literature and Broadway plays and movie reviews. We do not need just the things that belong to Christ—we need Christ Himself! We need to know Him personally and individually.

The Roman soldier had what belonged to Christ—the robe He wore, but he never knew the Lord Jesus, as far as we know. Are you absolutely sure you belong to Christ? Are you a part of the family of God? Have you had the new birth?

I was born on January 30, 1939, into a family named Smith. Ten years later, in 1949, I was born into a family called the family of God. Just as a physical birth brought me into this world, the spiritual birth brought me into the realm of living with Jesus Christ. Have you had that spiritual birth? All of the possessions of Christ mean nothing unless you yourself have him personally.

II. He Chose a Secondhand Reality

Not only did the Roman soldier choose a secondhand robe, he also chose a secondhand reality. The soldier's second mistake was to take the possessions of Jesus' life rather than the purchase of His death.

When I pastored in Warren, Arkansas, I met a lady who kept an unusual array of clothes for years. One night her husband came in and, as was his habit, he put the clothes he was going to wear the next day on the back of a chair in his bedroom. I have seen that very arrangement of clothes: trousers placed over the back of the chair; shirt and suspenders on the chair; and beneath that chair, shoes and a pair of socks.

During the night that man died. That woman, because of her superstition, did not let a soul move those clothes. She still lives in that house and still sleeps in that bedroom, and those clothes are still where her husband left them more than twenty-five years ago.

It is amazing how people have superstitions about what belongs to Christ. They emphasize, "Now, Preacher, we need to be very quiet in church. Preacher, we need to treat the Bible very reverently." I agree with them. Even though they would never use the word "superstition," some people have weird fixations about what belongs to Christ.

This Roman soldier chose a secondhand reality when he won that robe. He was enjoying one of the possessions of the life of Christ.

There are three areas where the life of Christ has been unusually influential.

A. Jesus Influences Social Concern

In the area of poverty, Jesus has told us to feed the poor. When Sandy and I were coming to First Southern in view of a call, we turned on the television that first Sunday morning and heard Evangelist Larry Jones preach, the first preacher I heard in Oklahoma. He is a member of our church, and I am grateful for his "Feed the Children" ministry across the world. He is doing a remarkable work for the Lord.

You may comment, "But, Preacher, we need to feed people's souls more than the bodies." I agree, but you plan to eat lunch today, don't you? You want to be fed, and so do I. Most of us eat too much, I would imagine. Jesus was concerned with the social needs of man, absolutely no question about it.

One Sunday, I stood in a boat on the Sea of Galilee and preached to the crowds. I looked over to my right and beheld those lovely trees and those lush, grassy slopes where one day Jesus took five loaves and two fish and fed 5,000 people. Jesus used physical miracles to point out spiritual lessons. I understand that. That is the same reason He taught in parables. Yet, I also know that Jesus fed people because they were hungry.

Jesus healed people because they were sick. Jesus raised people because they were dead. He restored people because they had been disenfranchised. Jesus loved people who were the objects of bigotry.

Through the centuries Jesus has helped us to be concerned with those around us. When I was at Del City I was so grateful to pastor a church that had never, as far as I know, in its history manifested bigotry and prejudice.

I remember when we had Willa Dorsey at Del City sometime ago. She and I are good friends, and she has sung in several of my "Real Evangelism" Crusades. Willa testified, "Now God made Bailey Smith, and God made me. I am his sister, and he is my brother, and we are close friends. God formed both of us. He cooked us both and made us human beings—He just left me in the oven a little bit longer than he left Brother Bailey!" I stood up and replied, "Willa Dorsey, that's right! In fact, when God looks at you, He is going to say, 'Well done!' "

Jesus has helped us see that we do not have a black

mankind, a red mankind, a yellow mankind, a brown mankind, and a white mankind—we have a human race! We become brothers and sisters when we are redeemed by the Cross. The common ground of man is not the color of his skin but the condition of his heart. When the blood has been shed on a person, regardless of race, they become brothers in the Lord Jesus Christ. Jesus was concerned about the physical and the spiritual and the mental and the emotional.

Perhaps you have heard of Clara Barton. She had a deep concern for those who had physical, emotional, and mental needs. She had an unbounded compassion. As she set up her organization, she said, "I will not have an organization unless it is represented by a cross." Someone suggested, "Clara Barton, it needs to be a certain kind of cross." She agreed, "It does—it needs to be a red cross." So, she called her organization, The Red Cross. The "red" stood for the bloody red cross of Jesus Christ. She explained, "As the Cross of Christ reaches down into the pits and brings men up to a new level, because of the blood of Jesus upon the Cross, the Red Cross will also reach out to those that need somebody to help them." The bloody red Cross of Calvary has inspired millions of people to be concerned about the social needs of others. I am grateful for the impact of Jesus in social concerns.

B.   Jesus Influences Moral Awareness

The life of Christ has also been influential in the area of moral awareness. When you become a Christian, you have a new moral standard. That standard is the life of Jesus. He lived an ethical, moral, circumspect life. He requires that from those who follow Him.

C. Jesus Influences World Vision

The life of Jesus not only brought out social concerns and moral awareness but also a world vision.

As you read the Bible you will notice how often the word "all" is there. *"All* power is given unto Me ..." "Ye shall be witnesses unto me both in Jerusalem, and in *all* Judea, and in Samaria, and unto the uttermost part of the earth." "For God so loved the world ..."—which encompasses all.

God gives a worldwide vision to those of us who have been born again.

Some years ago I was in Nairobi, Kenya, in East Africa. I stood in a place called the Methari Valley where homes by the hundreds would break your heart. One feature of the area was the poor sewage system. In a Methari Valley home the only sanitary facility was just a little trough at one end of the house. All of the sewage was deposited there.

It then flowed from the house into an open gutter in the street. There is stench about it. The garbage, the sewage, the filth breaks your heart. To take a deep breath would literally hurt your eyes, ears, nose, and throat. You would choke if you did so.

I stood on a hill with Dr. Adams, one of our Southern Baptist missionaries, and looked out across that Methari Valley in which he ministered. I thought to myself, *The life of Jesus said we are to love those people, to care for those people, to minister to them in the name of God.* Sad to admit it, but there are areas in our own country with problems almost as bad as the Methari Valley.

We must not make the same mistake the Roman soldier made. He was so engrossed with the possession of Jesus, the robe, that he missed the person of Jesus. He never once was purchased by the death of Christ, to the best of our knowledge.

The greatest message of the church is what Jesus did with His death. Jesus took our death, our judgment, our hell. If you will trust in Christ, then one day you will not have to die and go to hell. You can be born again. What a glorious truth!

III. He Chose a Secondhand Relationship

Not only did the Roman soldier choose a secondhand robe and a secondhand reality, he also chose a secondhand relationship. The soldier received from others instead of discovering for himself, a tragic mistake!

Picture him as he came to the Cross and found his fellow soldiers casting lots for the robe of Christ. He asked, "What are you guys doing?" His fellow soldiers responded, "We are casting lots to see who gets what belonged to Jesus—this seamless robe. We have never seen a robe like this!" "Let me get in on it," he insisted. Since he happened to be a good gambler, the Roman soldier won what belonged to others and what originally had belonged to Christ.

So many people have a problem en route to the Cross. They stop by and visit with others. They receive what belonged to Christ secondhand, instead of going to Jesus for themselves.

Many people's Christianity could be described in two words: gatherings and movements. "Hey, did you hear that Brother Shabiwabi was in town last night?"

"Oh, I wondered where you were."

"I went over to hear Brother Shabiwabi 'do his thing' at that church across town. You should have been there!"

"Brother Bailey, have you heard the new Kenneth Higginbotham records?"

"No."

"Have you heard Oral Humbard's new message?"

"No."

"Oh, listen! Have you been to Dr. Whistlebritches's latest seminar on how to be prosperous?"

"No."

"Have you heard Professor Bottletop?"

"No."

"Have you heard Ernest Angletree?"

"No. "Have you heard Bailey Smith . . . ?" Listen, do not pick up your theology from Bailey Smith. Get it from the Word of God. Don't ever become so enamored with a personality that you forget the Person of Jesus Christ. Don't ever get so enraptured with a man's slant that you forget the Scripture!

Two times in my life my ministry could have been ruined by men whom I loved and appreciated. Those two occasions would have thrown me off track in two ways: I would have had a misunderstanding of the power and function of the Holy Spirit and of the person of Jesus Christ. Many men who preach the Bible are dead wrong in those two areas.

If there is one man on earth God wants you to be influenced by, of course, it is your shepherd—your pastor. But even he could be wrong on occasions. However, do not let anyone influence you to the point that you become like the Roman soldier and stop too long so you never get to Jesus all for yourself.

Certainly God wants you to have someone who feeds you spiritually, who guides you, who influences you to grow in the grace and admonition of the Lord. Jesus looked at one of His disciples when he had misunderstood Jesus' ministry, and inquired, "Have I been so long with you, and yet hast thou not known me . . . ?"

In Matthew 16:17, after Simon Peter confessed Jesus as "the Christ, the Son of the living God," Jesus answered him, "Simon . . . flesh and blood hath not revealed [this] unto thee, but my Father which is in heaven." The best teaching you will ever receive in this life will not come from the preaching of Bailey Smith, Jimmy Swaggart, Bill Gothard, or some other man of God. It will come when you fall on your knees alone before Almighty God and God fills you with His holy presence. The Word of God will be revealed to you by the Spirit of God, who will empower you to come up off of your knees a new man or a new woman, with a new zeal from God. It is good to have Christian preachers, workers, musicians, but the greatest thing you will ever do is go to the Cross all by yourself! Get to Jesus, get to the foot of the Cross, and do not stop with people along the way.

IV. He Chose a Secondhand Rationale

The Roman soldier chose a secondhand robe, a secondhand reality, and a secondhand relationship. Last of all, he chose a secondhand rationale. He made the mistake of avoiding the weak and focusing on the strong.

Do you realize that God almost never does the obvious? A preacher in the Old Testament needed to be straightened out, Balaam. God did not call together a committee of great prophets. What did God use? An ass! There came a time when Saul needed to be told he was a liar. What did God use? The bellowing of a sheep! Simon Peter needed to be told he was a compromiser. What did God use? A rooster!

The Roman soldier saw some strong men with swords, shields, and armor. He thought, *I want to be identified with those people.* I do not want to be identified with a dying, weak, emaciated Nazarene.

Today it sometimes seems the work of the church is losing. It sometimes seems the world and its affairs are successful and influential. Look at the church, and it often seems to be anemic and antiseptic. However, the work of Jesus is the only one that will last forever and forever.

If you are not careful, you will attach yourself with the apparent strength of this world, but it will be to your eternal weakness. The Roman soldier made a horrible, gross error: he associated with the strength of the military, and he missed the power of eternal life.

Dear friend, I pray God will help you see what is real, what is lasting, what is strong, and what is genuinely good.

A family visited New York City because they had always wanted to see a Broadway Play. They had told their friends in Texas they would see "Fiddler On The Roof." When they arrived, the only night they could go, it was sold out. They begged the man at the ticket counter to let them in, but he appologized, "I'm sorry, we don't even have standing room. You can't get in!"

When it was over, those people were still there. They watched the people as they came out and asked them, "How was it? Was 'Fiddler on the Roof' good?" One man, coming out of the theater, threw his ticket stubs onto the sidewalk. The man from Texas, standing near there with his wife, reached down to the sidewalk and picked up the ticket stubs.

They returned home, and someone excitedly asked, "How was 'Fiddler on the Roof'?" The man answered, "Look at these attractive tickets. These are the stubs from 'Fiddler on the Roof.'" "Was it good?" they asked. "Yes, it was good!" "Did everybody seem to enjoy it?" "Yes, I believe everybody in the theater enjoyed it." Yet, they had never gotten in!

I have discovered that many people in the church have only the torn stubs of someone else's experiences. They have never entered the Kingdom for themselves. God wants you to have more than another's experiences. He wants you to experience Jesus all for yourself.

Almighty God declared, "My thoughts are not your thoughts, neither are your ways my ways." While you may have Jesus all around you, my desire for your heart is that you have Jesus inside of you!

9

The Cross and Compassion

And as Moses lifted up the serpent in the wilderness, even so must the Son of man be lifted up: That whosoever believeth in him should not perish, but have eternal life. For God so loved the world, that he gave his only begotten Son, that whosoever believeth in him should not perish, but have everlasting life. For God sent not his Son into the world to condemn the world; but that the world through him might be saved. He that believeth on him is not condemned; but he that believeth not is condemned already, because he hath not believed in the name of the only begotten Son of God. And this is the condemnation, that light is come into the world, and men loved darkness rather than light, because their deeds were evil. For every one that doeth evil hateth the light, neither cometh to the light, lest his deeds should be reproved. But he that doeth truth cometh to the light, that his deeds may be made manifest, that they are wrought in God. (John 3:14-21).

After I was graduated from Ouachita Baptist College, a college friend of mine went to a place we used to call the low water bridge. Coming back, he had a terrible accident as a pickup truck was traveling on the wrong side of the gravel road. It struck my friend's little Volkswagen head-on. The only person injured was my friend as the steering

column of his car struck his chest and pinned him against
the seat. It was a tragic moment. He called out, "Please,
somebody, go get some help! We have got to get to the
Clark County Hospital."

The other boy in the car ran to the road, flagged down
a lady in her luxury automobile, and told her the problem.
She could see the pickup truck and the little Volkswagen
on the other side of it.

"Ma'am, if you will hurry, I believe we can get my
friend to the Clark County Hospital." She pressed the
electric button of the window, and a little air-conditioning
flew out into the face of this scared boy. She replied,
"Young man, I don't want to get involved." She rolled her
window back up, and down the highway toward Hot
Springs she continued. That young man behind the
wheel, whom I believe would be preaching to thousands
of people this very day, is now with the Lord. His life's
blood was pumped out onto the floor of that little car
because a lady did not want to become involved.

As I go across this country, I discover that not many
people really care whether people live or die. They do not
care whether churches succeed or fail, do not care about
some of the basic moral and social issues of our country.
That is why immorality is running rampant. People simply do not care.

Eleven men stood in New York City and watched a
woman being raped. No one intervened. One of those
men later being questioned was asked, "Why didn't you
help?" He alibied, "I didn't know the woman." That was
his only response.

At Del City we were gravely hurt when one of the men
in our church, a policeman, was murdered as two men
accosted him while he was on duty. Spectators watched,
but no one came to the aid of the policeman. He is now
dead because no one was willing to help.

In a bathroom of a filling station near Chicago, a suicide note was left under the dead body of a teenage girl. The note read, "Momma, you don't care—just like nobody else cares for me. P. S. Tell my rotten Daddy, I'll see him in hell!"

Let me ask you a personal question: do you care? Do you really care? Does it bother you, does it concern you that this world is in dire need?

Frankly, as I go around preaching from church to church, I do not discover many Baptists who really care. You can plead your heart out for them to be back on Monday night of a revival—they won't come. You can tell them the financial needs of a particular effort—but they don't give. You can tell them about a lost world that is going to hell—but they don't show up to visit. No one seems to care.

It is rare to find someone who shows a forehead with concern, eyes with compassion, and a heart that beats to meet the needs of those around them.

A lady, obviously ready to deliver a baby, tried two places in Oklahoma City, but no one would let her in. Finally, on that cold November day, she gave birth on a sidewalk in our city. Eventually, one woman ran to a neighbor and got a blanket. People gawked at the woman who had no place to go and had to deliver her baby on a cold sidewalk. No one seemed to care.

However, I have good news! God does care! Jesus does care! The example of the Cross of Christ is: we must care!

C. S. Lewis wrote, "A man is no more to be blamed for his lack of compassion than for his blond hair." When I first read that statement I thought, *You know, that cannot be true.*

I suppose, however, it is true. I have known some people who are very sensitive, who weep easily, who seem to have feelings of empathy towards others without much

effort. Then I have seen others who are just like bulldogs
—quick to gnash, speedy to critize, swift to find fault, and
fast to be insensitive to the hurts and concerns of others.

C. S. Lewis went on to write, "Even though a man may
not have in him a desire to help and have in him, as a
natural part of his life, compassion, he *must* care, because
he is commanded to care by his Lord." So you and I *must*
care whether or not we feel like it. We have to care to
care, because Jesus taught we are supposed to.

From our text, I notice at least five reasons why I must
care for the people around me. One of the rarest qualities
I find in a preacher, a deacon, a Christian woman, a Christian man, a Christian staff member is the ingredient of
compassion. I have seen men on church staffs who are
good administrators—good with money, good with numbers, good with business, good with organization. Yet it is
rare to locate a man who has a heart, who has compassion
for the souls of men and women. Let me suggest five
reasons why the Cross tells us we ought to care for those
around us.

I. I Must Care Because of Mankind's Need

Mankind has a sin problem that can only be answered
by what Jesus did on the Cross. The Bible asserts that
when sin entered into man, man was no longer level but
uneven. He became off balance. The Bible says his mind,
body, and soul became at enmity with God. All of a sudden man was at variance with his Creator. A great gap, "a
great gulf" was fixed between man and his God. That
chasm was brought about by man's sin, by man's rebellion
against God.

Mankind has a desperate need because its mind is
mixed up. It is confused. The Bible says in 2 Thessalonians
that God allowed some people to be so deluded that they
believed a lie. All around us are people who do not know

right from wrong. Why? Because they have allowed Satan so much control of their lives they do not know how to make the right decisions. They do not understand how to choose right from wrong, good from bad, high standards from low.

That is why Paul wrote to that church in Thessalonica that God has literally deluded their minds so they could believe a lie (see 2 Thess. 2:11-12). That is hard to understand, but it is a Scriptural truth.

When I think about what sin has done to the thinking of man, I cannot help but think about the alcoholic beverage industry. Through the years the liquor people have lied to us.

All across the nation the liquor proponents have used deception to grab the votes of naïve, gullible people, so they made it appear it would be safer if we had liquor-by-the-drink. State after state fell to the liquor lobby. Mark my word and see if I am not a prophet of truth: Oklahoma in the future will have many alcohol-related deaths and more alcohol-related crime. That is so all over.

Perhaps you are thinking, *Well, Preacher, I just do not believe that!* It was interesting that one county which voted "no" was the only county that had legalized gambling. The reporters interviewed one man and asked him, "Now that you have horse racing, why did you vote against liquor?" He replied, "Gamblers are enough! We don't want drunk gamblers!" Good response!

Do you realize that since the beginning of World War II, 520,000 Americans have died in combat in a war somewhere in the world. That is a staggering total. We regret all of those deaths, but at the same time 800,000 people have died on the highways of our nation because of alcohol!

Many of us lost friends and relatives during the Vietnam War. Some 39,000 Americans were killed during the entire American involvement in Vietnam. Yet more Americans are killed in alcohol-related deaths each year than were killed in all the years we were in Vietnam! Incredible!

In fact, it has been proven that a young man, ages 18-24, was safer in Saigon than in one hundred U.S. cities on a Friday or Saturday night.

When man if full of sin his mind is twisted. His evaluations are wrong. His understanding is not what it ought to be. I find it incredible, and the legal people are having a good time with it, that the two homosexuals who are accused of slaughtering those five people at the Geronimo, Oklahoma, bank, have now said they cannot testify against each other because they are married!

That sin is repulsive to Almighty God, and God hates it! However, I want to tell you why those two homosexuals became what they became, why we have the growing problems of immorality we have right now—no one cared!

The liquor people spent $250,000 in six weeks to convince Oklahomans to vote "yes"—and we voted "Yes"! Now we are going to reap the rewards of it. The reporters interviewed me and asked, "What do you think is going to happen now in the state of Oklahoma with the churches since we voted in gambling and liquor?" I answered, "I'll tell you what we'll do: the churches will clean up the messes that you voted in! The churches will be there loving the people who lost their money down at the racetrack. We will be there loving the people who lost their loved ones because of alcohol. We will be comforting the families that had a little child struck by an automobile driven by a drinking teenager. We will be willing to keep loving and caring for people!"

Even though they will not listen to us, the real churches are still going to be there picking up humanity. Why?

Because we care. If there is any reason why you and I must care, it is because of the profound need we see in men and women around us. They need us. The very reason Jesus died upon the Cross is the sin nature of mankind. He knew that man had no solution other than His death upon the Cross.

What has always plagued me and mystified me is man's inhumanity to man. Man is by nature a sinner. Man is by nature evil.

I remember when I was a small boy, my father had bought some books about World War II from *Life* magazine. I used to sit on our couch and look at those books. They stunned me because they showed piles of bodies, tanks running over bodies as if the bodies were nothing but debris. They pictured people running out of foxholes on fire as the flame throwers would strike them.

I remember, even as an immature child, thinking: *How could men be so cruel to other men? How could men hurt others so much?* That is the nature of man. That is why man needs plenty of care. By his very nature, he will do evil.

When I was in high school there was a big boy who had freckles as big as silver dollars and bright red hair. He was tough, and everyone in school called him "The Greeter." When a boy moved in, "The Greeter" would go over and greet the boy by giving him "a fat lip." I remember one time I objected, and he gave me a fat lip. He loved to hit people in the mouth. That was the joy of his life, and he was good at it. He had gotten a lot of practice! I thought, *How can a guy be so insensitive?*

Then I pick up the Word of God, and I read what Jesus did when people were in deep need. You remember that woman who was caught in the very act of adultery. She was dragged out into the streets, and the men stood around her ready to stone her. Jesus, of course, suggested that those without sin could cast the first stone—but He also took His finger and began to write in the sand.

We do not know what He wrote, but many assume that He began to write the names, and also perhaps the besetting sins, of the men who were standing around that woman. Perhaps they knew that He knew they had been her customers or paramours. Maybe they knew He knew they would like to stone her to death because, if she lived, she might let their wives know where they were last Saturday night. I have learned that people who are eager to condemn often are trying to hide something in their own lives. How eager they were to condemn and to destroy that woman—and to be rid of her.

What did Jesus do? He came to her aid, while all of the other men were ready to stone her. It is refreshing when the whole world is against you, and someone comes to your aid.

Sometime ago, Dr. Jimmy Draper made a controversial statement. The reporters called me and asked, "What do you think about that?" My first thought was, *Now, Bailey, if you agree with him, you are going to catch it on the chin!* Then my second thought was, *You know, when I made a controversial statement, all my friends were logical and sensible, and it made me mad because they protected themselves.*

So, I thought: *since Jimmy Draper is one of my best friends, I am going to stand with him.* I said to the reporters, "Well, I would just like to say one thing: I agree with him!" Boy, did I ever get it on the chin and everywhere else! Yet, I believe that was the right thing, because: number one, he was right, and number two, it is good to stand with someone who needs someone to stand with them.

One day I may be in trouble, and I will need your support. One day you may be in trouble, and you will need me to visit you, help you, and strengthen you. That was the nature of Jesus. Anytime Jesus found somebody that the crowd was eager to condemn, He came, gave them a second chance, and asked to be their friend.

Remember the money changers in the Temple. Jesus did hate the money changers. Rather, He loved them. He ran the money changers out because of what they were doing. People would bring in foreign currency, and the money changers would change the foreign money to Temple money.

When Jesus saw them take, for instance, a dollar of foreign money and exchange it for forty cents of Temple money, it angered Him that people were being deceived and robbed. His actions were not in hatred of the money changers but in love and defense for the people who were being cheated. That is still the personality of Jesus.

When little children were brought to Jesus, they climbed onto His lap. The disciples came and said, "Shhhh! Get away, leave Him alone!" Jesus replied, "Wait a minute, I want these little children. It is better for a man to have a millstone tied around his neck and be drowned in the sea, than to chase a little child from Me. Let them stay!"

Through the years I have advised our staff, when a little child comes up to them, to get down on their level. Do not stand over them and look down on them as if you are Goliath. One day, that child is going to grow up and he is going to realize someone cared.

One of the reasons I know you and I must care is: the Cross teaches us, by the very fact Jesus had to die, that we are deep sinners with a profound need. Man needs to be loved, or his sin will dominate his life. We must love him out of it.

II. I Must Care Because of Man's Worth

Not only must I care because of mankind's need but also because of its worth. That is the paradoxical nature of the Cross. On the one hand the Cross shows how evil man is that God's Son would have to die for him, but it also shows how valuable man is that Jesus would do precisely that. What a paradox! That Jesus would die on the Cross in man's stead, in man's behalf, demonstrates the unbelievable value of mankind.

Every now and then I hear about an antique car being sold for a million dollars. Or perhaps people will go to the Derby to view millions of dollars worth of horse flesh.

I am amazed at how many people are spending thousands of dollars on dolls. I was in a home not long ago where the lady had over a thousand dolls. In every room were dolls of every size. I could not believe it! I have never seen so much money being spent on hobbies.

If an antique car or a race horse can be worth a million dollars or more, can you imagine how valuable you are when you are worth a Cross? God saw you and loved you a whole Cross's worth? Jesus bled and died for you?

All of our righteousness is as filthy rags (see Isa. 64:6). As Paul put it, in me there is no clean thing—but that is from my perspective! From the perspective of God, from the view of heaven, God looked down upon you and me and saw that we were worthy of the death of his Son. But— "For by grace are ye saved through faith; and that not of yourselves; it is the gift of God . . ." (Eph. 2:8).

Jesus loves us so much, He cares for us so much. Why? Because a person is worth so much that God's Son would die upon the Cross for him (see Mark 8:36-37).

A discouraged preacher, who later became famous, one time was going to commit suicide. He stood on the brink of a bridge ready to jump into the water. As he started to jump, he remembered the gist of a sermon: "Destroy not the life for whom Jesus died! Destroy not the life for whom Jesus died!" He could not take his own life. The worst horror of suicide and murder is that you destroy a life for whom Jesus died!

I was in Texas sometime ago in a city-wide crusade. I was talking with a preacher, and I even hate to tell this story. I remarked to him, "Man, many of your churches in this area are not growing!" He replied, "I know it." I said, "There are people everywhere. Why don't you grow?" Then he floored me: "Preacher, if we really grew as we should, we would have to reach a bunch of Mexicans!"

I came back with, "Friend, we have Mexican people in our church, and they are some of our best members. We have black people in our church, and they are such wonderful people. We even have a few decent white people in our church! They are all welcome, whether they are rich or poor, regardless of their skin color!" Jesus did not die for pigmentation of skin. He died for the souls of mankind. The ground is level at the foot of the Cross. Whosoever will may come! Jesus died on the Cross because every person has inestimable worth.

III. I Must Care Because of Mankind's Ignorance

I must care not only because of man's need and worth but also because of man's ignorance. I am utterly amazed how illiterate this country is concerning the Word of God. Even though I don't agree with all I see on Christian television, I am grateful for those on TV who preach the truth of God's Word because this country is biblically illiterate. They simply do not understand the Word of God.

There are three areas where mankind has been ignorant:

A. Mankind Is Ignorant of the Atonement

People have been ignorant about the substitutionary death of Jesus on the Cross. One time I stood on a street corner in New York City and asked everyone who would listen to me if they understood what Jesus did on the Cross. Only one man in an hour could tell me the truth about the Cross.

It would be the same all across America, even in the "Bible Belt." They do not understand that "without the shedding of blood there is no remission of sin."

This country must be cared for now as never before, because we have often tolerated a bunch of namby-pamby preachers who do not speak the whole truth, who thus compromise the Word of God, who put a question mark around the miraculous, and who have seldom, if ever, preached on the Cross! Many have never taken the Word of God and rightly divided it.

Right now this country needs unusual care and compassion from blood-bought people who believe that the only hope for this country is understanding the Word of God. That is the only hope we have ever had! There is ignorance of the vicarious death of Jesus upon the Cross.

B. Man is Ignorant of Forgiveness

Second, man is ignorant of the permanent forgiveness of sin. I was preaching at Rehoboth Baptist Church in Atlanta sometime ago. While I was signing some Bibles after church, the music director requested, "Brother Smith, can you talk to this man? He does not believe what I am telling him."

I signed a few more Bibles and then talked to the man. "What's the problem?" I asked. He said, "Well, I don't believe what you said." I inquired, "Why do you want to talk to me some more if I am a liar." His answer was, "I want you to explain it in case I misunderstood you." I then asked, "What is it you don't believe?"

He expressed himself, "I don't believe this automatic stuff."

"Automatic stuff? What is that?" I came back.

"Well, Jesus died on the Cross, and we ask for forgiveness of our sins, and automatically we are forgiven. Do you believe what you said, that we are automatically forgiven?" "Yes, it is automatic!"

"Do you really believe that?"

"Yes, I believe it because it's true—you are automatically forgiven when you repent and turn from your sins."

He went on, "Man, if you knew what I have done, you wouldn't say that."

"I don't need to know what you've done, I just know what Jesus has done! 'Where sin did abound, grace did much more abound!' "

Now I would love to end this successfully but I cannot. The man would never accept Christ. I thought I answered his arguments well, but he refused. I have discovered what the problem is with a man like that. It was not that he could not accept the forgiveness of God—the problem is that he did not want it! The reason why is because he still had sin in his life that he wanted to keep. He knew he was dirty and rotten, and he knew that God would not forgive him without repentance.

People have bypassed the truth that once you have asked forgiveness, once you have repented, once you have experienced the new birth, once you have been indwelt by the Holy Spirit, your sins are forgiven. You say, "Well, Bailey Smith, if I believed like that, I would just get saved and then live like the devil!"

No, you won't. A person who wants to live like the devil is of the devil! If you have ever been saved, that will not be your attitude. You will never say, "Well, I'll just get

saved, then live like the devil, and go to heaven one day."
That will never happen. Jesus forgives your sins once and
for all—automatically—when you ask forgiveness and repent and turn from them, but also remember the Bible
says, "Old things are passed away, behold all things are
become new" (2 Cor. 5:17b). You become a new creature,
a new creation, in Jesus Christ.

C.   Mankind Is Ignorant of Transformation

Third, man is ignorant of how different he can be when
Jesus changes his life. He is ignorant of the transformed
life. I listened as Iris Urrey Blue spoke to First Southern
Baptist at Del City. It is wonderful how God has changed
that woman's life. She had been into everything from
dope to prostitution; she had been in prison. She had been
crude, crass, and gutter-like. If there was a sin to commit,
she had probably done it. Yet, she turned out to be a lady
because God changed her life! She was gloriously transformed. Man is ignorant of Jesus' transforming power.

Not long ago at an airport I saw two celebrities who
were traveling together en route to Oklahoma to perform
for a function in our state. I could see they were trying not
to be recognized, so I tried to recognize them a little bit.
I went over to one of them and shook his hand. He was
gracious and talked to me. He didn't act as if he were put
out with me, so we talked a while.

We boarded the plane, and for some reason I had been
upgraded. I never, never fly first class but was assigned a
seat right across the aisle from them. It surprised me, and
it surely surprised them, so we began to share, and I told
them about my ministry; they told me about their background.

Later, they got into an argument. Quite often you can
see these people on television, but I have never heard
such crude, coarse, and bitter language. Their eyes had

seemed glassy, even when I had talked with them before emplaning. I thought to myself: *Here they are, well-known and making loads of money, but they have missed life so miserably!*

When the plane landed, I fell to my knees and put my right hand on this guy's left knee. I looked at both of them and said, "I overheard your conversation (they dropped their heads a little bit), and I want to tell you there is a better life for you guys. With your background you know what it is. I want to remind you that, if you ever want to repent, there is a preacher who told you the greatest life is the one Jesus Christ can give you. You don't have to be bitter; you don't have to use vile language. You don't have to be mad at anyone. You can be full of joy and full of love. You are going to make some mistakes in your line of work. You are going to be tempted to do some horrible things and make some compromises, but don't do it!"

One of them replied, "Now, Bailey Boy, we're going to do this, but I want to tell you now that we are going to do it in our own way." I did not let that pass. I answered, "No, you can only do it God's way. You cannot do it your own way."

You see, the hardest thing for man to do is die. The message of the Cross is: the only way to have life is to die. Jesus talked about the abundant life. Yet there are Christians out there who have eternal life, but they do not have abundant life. You reap abundant life by every day letting more of yourself die—more of your wishes, more of your habits, more of your inconsistencies, more of those sins that quench the Holy Spirit. Let the Spirit expel the barriers from your life, and then you will have the abundant life. If you want life, it all comes through death! (see Gal. 2:20; Col. 3:3).

Those two celebrities may never know life because they are hanging onto mere baubles, and they want to "do it their way." The only way you can ever have the abundant life is by sincerely praying, "God, I don't know what I have to do, but I'm willing to do it." When you come to that point, God will fill you so full of Jesus that you will not have any room for garbage.

IV. I Must Care Because of Mankind's Desperation

Not only must I care for man because of his need, his worth, and his ignorance but because of his desperation.

That is why mankind goes after mere religion. Remember that every concoction of the occult and every configuration of religion is not man's search for God. It is man's attempt to find a substitute for God. Why do we have artificial sugar?—to avoid sugar. Why do we have artificial salt?—to avoid salt. Why do we have Astroturf?—to avoid grass. Why do we have religion?—to avoid salvation! The pseudo-intellectual, that false mind, out in the world says: "I want this cult, and I want that religion because it appeals to me. This stuff of heaven and hell, repentance, the blood on the Cross, and Jesus' coming again—that is far too simple."

In the world there is no new revelation, there is no new doctrine, there is no new salvation. Only the way of the Cross will suffice. Only the blood leads home. It is the way of repentance, the way of being saved, the way of the new birth, the way of life eternal!

Let all the religions and all the cults arise. Let all the appeals to one's intellect and all the enticements that gratify one's aesthetic mind enter.

They will come and go. When people bypass the Bible, the gospel, and the doctrine of the Cross, they have lost it! The only way to God is the narrow way. "Neither is there salvation in any other [name] . . ." (Acts 4:12).

People need our compassion, because they do not even understand how desperately lost they are. There is only one hope for them. "I am the Way, the Truth, and the Life," declared the Lord Jesus (see John 14:6).

V. I Must Care Because of Mankind's Immortality

I must care for man because of his need, his worth, his ignorance, and his desperation. Finally, I must care because of his immortality. A fine Christian man remarked sometime ago, "Preacher, have you ever had any doubts?"

I replied, "Yes, Sir."

"I mean, doubts about the Bible."

"Sure."

"Well, I have been doubting something lately. I have been doubting heaven."

"Well, tell me about it."

He continued, "You know, I go to a funeral. I look in the casket, and that guy is not in heaven. There he is! He is right there. Same hands, same face, same body that I have seen all the time I have known the guy, and I think, *That guy is not in heaven, he is in that casket.*"

I replied, "The Bible never says you take that body to heaven anyway. You get rid of that body, and God gives you a new body."

"But there he is—let's face it."

"OK. Do you believe in Jesus?"

"Oh, yes, I am saved."

"Do you believe that Jesus died on the Cross and shed His blood?"

"Yes."

"Do you believe in hell?"

"I believe in hell because I know a lot of people who ought to go there."

I said, "Let me tell you why you can believe in heaven. God never would have allowed His Son to die for something that was going to die."

"I never thought of that."

"That's right, God would be a tyrant and a cruel Father if He let His Son die for something that was going to die!"

Man has an immortal soul. God breathed into man the breath of life and man became a living soul. That soul is eternal and lives forever in heaven or in hell. Jesus died that all people might be saved, that all might have eternal life.

It reminded me of that time in Clinton, Louisiana, when a very bitter man said to me, "Preacher, I am bitter towards our country because my boy died in Vietnam. My wife and I have been brokenhearted not only because he was our only son, but what really hurt me was that he died for something he didn't save!"

The cruelty of Vietnam is not that we were there. The cruelty of Vietnam is that we did not win! The boys died in vain, because the politicians listened to longhaired rebels on our streets, rather than looking at the future benefit of that country—and ours. God help us!

If a father would be mad because his boy died and what he died for is under a dictatorship, I wonder how God felt when Jesus died for people and some of them say, "Well, I think all you need is baptism and good works and ritualism."

Jesus, the Son of God, died for you. The reason I have to care for people is because every man, every woman, every boy, and every girl is going to live somewhere forever. Each one is an immortal soul. They are going to stand before God and, my friend, you are, too.

Some years ago a bus full of college football players was coming down on Monarch Pass at the Continental Divide. It is 11,000 feet high, and at Monarch Pass it drops 4,000 feet within five miles. As they drove through that area, the brakes of the bus went out, sending the bus careening down the mountainside.

The football players would shift their weight to one side, and then to the other at a key word from the bus driver. That kept the bus on those hairpin curves all the way down that mountain side.

Finally, the bus hit a stretch of level ground and almost collided with several cars coming from side streets. Three miles later, the bus came to a stop. You can imagine the relief. A reporter on board the bus asked the guys, "What was on your mind while you were coming down that mountain?" One player finally confessed it was an obscene magazine he had been reading. He confessed he didn't want to stand before God with that in his hand.

When I read the account of that runaway bus, I thought: *The one thing people must understand is that they are immortal and that they are going to stand before God in some condition.*

The best way to stand before God is redeemed, bought by the blood of Christ, saved, cleansed, Spirit-filled, abundantly living. The alternative is dreadful even to consider!

The Cross and compassion. We must care for our fellow human beings because of the example of Jesus on the Cross!

10

The Convincing Power of
the Cross

And, behold, the veil of the temple was rent in twain from the top to the bottom; and the earth did quake, and the rocks rent; And the graves were opened; and many bodies of the saints which slept arose. And came out of the graves after his resurrection, and went into the holy city, and appeared unto many. Now when the centurion, and they that were with him, watching Jesus, saw the earthquake, and those things that were done, they feared greatly, saying, Truly this was the Son of God (Matt. 27:51-54).

The Bible does not give us many facts about activities of the centurions. In fact, centurions are referred to only four times in the Bible.

Matthew 8 records the story where the centurion asked for his servant to be healed. "Master, I do not consider myself worthy enough for you to come under my roof, but would you just speak the word that my servant might live?" Jesus remarked that never before in Israel had He found such faith as possessed by that centurion.

Of course the most famous centurion of all was Cornelius. In the Book of Acts, he was a man of valiant prayer who sought God through Christ. Cornelius became a believer after his encounter with the Apostle Peter.

Acts 27 records a centurion by the name of Julius whom the Apostle Paul encountered on his voyage to Rome.

All three of the Synoptic Gospels record the reclamation of the centurion at the foot of the Cross. The account in Luke is somewhat different from the accounts in Matthew and Mark. The reason why this is so will be apparent as you read this chapter.

What was a centurion? A centurion had another name called a legionnaire. A legionnaire, the commander of one hundred men, a unit in the Roman Army known as a century, was called a Centurion. Over these men, he had absolute authority.

Publius, a first-century historian, said that in order to be a centurion one had to have unusually high intelligence and physical stamina.

From such a group as this would be chosen to lead other men, a special man who had a charisma about him. If one were chosen to be a centurion, he was the elite of a chosen few. The centurion was that kind of a man.

Why did the centurion become convinced that Jesus was indeed the Son of God? Why did he become convinced that Jesus was a good man? Subsequent history indicates that this man became a Christian. He accepted Christ, confessed him, and followed Him in all matters. I trust that is so.

Believer, have you ever thought about why you are a Christian? Why are you not a skeptic? Why are you not an atheist? Why are you not a Madelyn Murray O'Hair?

Why do you believe this Bible is true? Why have you chosen to believe that Jesus is Who He says He is?

Why have you chosen to believe? Why did this man choose to believe? What inspired and motivated him? What caused him to shout in a doxology of praise, "Truly this was the Son of God!'"? If anything will convince you that Jesus is all He said He is, surely it is the experience of the Cross.

There are four reasons why I believe the centurion burst out with, "Truly this was the Son of God!"

I. The Righteousness of Christ

The centurion could see the obvious goodness of Jesus Christ.

Luke 23:47 records that the centurion said, "Certainly this was a righteous man." You may think this is in contradiction with what is recorded in Matthew and Mark. The truth of the matter is that there is no contradicition. In essence what he exclaimed was, "Truly this was the Son of God, a righteous man!" He stated both of those.

What made him see the goodness of Jesus Christ? While the other people were hating, Jesus was loving. Those who passed by were railing at Him, but Jesus was blessing. One of the two thieves was pronouncing damnation upon the executioners, but Jesus was asking for their forgiveness. "He could have called ten thousand angels," but He did not.

There was a look about His facial countenance which showed He cared. He looked down from the Cross at His mother. He beheld John and asked John to take care of His mother. He then asked His mother to care for John.

Even when His mouth was as dry as sand, even when blood was spurting from His hands and feet, even when the thorns on His head were piercing His forehead and scalp, causing Him excruciating pain—Jesus still thought about others.

Mark records that the centurion was standing opposite Jesus, which meant that he was right there very close. He literally had a bird's-eye view of the crucifixion. He observed Jesus' character as He was being crucified. When those two thieves were thrown on the Cross they resisted and struggled as the nails were placed into their hands and feet. Yet when the Roman soldiers grabbed the Lord Jesus to nail Him on to the Cross, He did not resist. Jesus plainly said, "You do not need to take My Life from Me—no man can do that! I lay it down freely!" They watched Jesus as He climbed upon that Cross and gave His life freely.

Artists, most of the time, have drawn the Cross incorrectly. They will show it fifteen or twenty feet in the air. The truth of the matter is that the feet of the person being crucified were only a foot or two off the ground. When the mob would come by, they could mock at the victim's nakedness. Sometimes they would use rods and hit various parts of the victim's body. They might tear his beard from his face or strike him with their fists.

I can imagine that as the centurion witnessed that being done to the thieves, he heard them cursing, their profane remarks, and every kind of ugly obscenity being hurled toward those who railed against the thieves. However, Jesus blessed the people and loved them.

Do you believe that Jesus had probably encountered this centurion before His death? No question about it, for every place Jesus went during His life, He drew a crowd. Sometimes five to ten thousand people would follow Him, and sometimes they demanded attention. Every time a crowd gathered, according to Roman law, the soldiers had to be there. This was due to the fact that the Roman Empire controlled Judea and Galilee as Roman provinces. Thus, the Jewish people, even though it was their country, were not self-governing. They were captives of the Roman Empire.

The enemies of Jesus began to plot against Him. That is why you find Annas, Caiaphas, and Herod all trying to get along with one another, even though each mistrusted the others. Yet they were more afraid of Jesus than they were of one another.

Pilate was certainly afraid of a Jewish outbreak. He saw nothing Jesus was guilty of according to Roman law. Yet he succumbed to the pressure of the crowd as they clamored for Jesus to be crucified. He had been told by Caesar not to do anything which would cause an insurrection.

Therefore, everywhere Jesus had gone during His ministry which drew a crowd, the authorities would be there. I can imagine that time and again during the ministry of Jesus this very centurion was present. There were never many centurions to begin with, so it is possible that this very centurion was a constant companion of Jesus.

I wonder if that man might have been there the day Jesus forgave the woman who was caught in the very act of adultery. He would have seen her as she was set free and may have found it hard to believe that Jesus did that.

I wonder if that same centurion had been assigned to Jesus when He went out on that grassy slope to preach to the multitudes. He would have seen five thousand people who needed food. He would have seen Jesus feed those people by performing an unusual miracle.

I wonder if he saw Jesus that time when the disciples were trying to shoo away the little children. He would have heard Jesus' words, "It is better for a millstone to be tied around your neck, and for you to be thrown into the depths of the sea, than for you not to let a little child come unto Me!" I wonder if by the time of the crucifixion this centurion already had evidence in his heart that this, indeed, was an unusual man.

I cannot think of a greater compliment one man could give another than, "You are a good man!" There is a great deal of difference between being a "nice guy" and being a good person.

Sometimes a "nice guy" will still cheat in business.

Sometimes a nice guy will like you. Sometimes a nice guy may know proper etiquette but not know how to be good. There is a difference in knowing how to hold your fork and how to hold your tongue! There is a difference in knowing how to open the door for your wife and how to open the door for all kinds of evil that might come into your life.

The reason the Roman soldier could scream out to those around him, "Truly, this was the Son of God!" is that through Jesus' life and through the experiences of His execution, this Roman soldier saw a vastly different life.

He saw a quality in Jesus Christ that made him say, recorded in the Book of Luke, "Certainly this was a righteous man!" He also saw something about the humanity of Jesus that caused him to know that Jesus was a good man.

When Paul was in a Roman prison writing the Book of Philippians, he declared in 1:12, "But I would ye should understand, brethren, that the things which happened unto me have fallen out rather unto the furtherance of the gospel."To Paul it really did not matter what happened to him, because the furtherance of the gospel had been benefited.

The goal of Jesus during His entire life was that God the Father be visible, that God be seen in Him. Therefore whether Jesus was cursed or hurt or even executed, His Godly manhood was going to be seen.

Take the goodness of Jesus Christ and look at how He lived. Look at his manhood and how He treated women, other men, His enemies, and those around Him. Watch Him love the little children. Watch Him be kind to people who did not deserve His kindness. As you look at the sweet spirit of Jesus, you will want to say as this centurion, "This Man has to be real! This Man has to be authentic!

This Man has to be genuine, because of the obvious goodness of His manhood!"

A dear black friend of mine preaches in Detroit. He was
raised in the South under the bigotry and prejudice of
that day. His mother and father had been killed by whites.
He lived with his grandmother and with his brother. One
night men dressed in white hoods—the Ku Klux Klan—
came to their home.

He said, "We were frightened because we knew there
had been an uproar in the community. They burst open
the little door of that rundown shack in the cotton field.
They came in, got my older brother, dragged him out into
the yard, put ropes under his armpits, and tied that rope
to the horn of a saddle. Then they dragged him down a
terrible rocky road, through the briar patch, and then
around the courthouse down at the city square. When
they got through with him, they brought his body back to
my grandmother's yard and threw him into the yard,
bloody and dying. He died before we could get him into
the house. Then the man in the white hood apologized
because they had gotten the wrong man!

"But they did not call him the wrong 'man'—they
called him another name some people have for blacks.
They called him a horrible thing, killed him, and then
said, 'I'm sorry, but we thought that boy was the one that
molested one of our white girls.' That was the way they
treated him. They murdered him and got by with it."

The next morning his grandmother got up to work at
the white folks' plantation house. She first cut some turnip
greens, then went back to the house and removed the salt
cloth from the meat.

That preacher friend of mine urged his grandmother,
"Grandma, you poison those white folks' food today!
When you cook for those white folks today, you put poison

in that food. Don't let them get by with what they have done to my brother!"

He will never forget how she disappeared down the road as she went to that plantation house, swept and mopped their floors, cared for their children, bathed their children, and cooked their three meals that day. Tired and worn out, she came back home that night, and he asked, "Grandma, did you poison the white folks' food like I asked you to do?"

She said, "Honey Chile, the Lord never told me to worry about what the white folks do. He just told me to worry about what I do! The Bible says that we are to love our enemies and to pray for those that despitefully use us. Today they saw that I lived like Jesus told me to live!"

When the goodness of Jesus comes into your life there is a difference about you. You don't just know proper etiquette; you don't just know how to say "Yes, Sir!" and "No, Ma'am!" You don't just know how to be polite. You don't just do the things society demands. There is a different nature inside you that makes you a truly good person!

A good man doesn't have to worry about what may be found out about himself. A good man doesn't do anything in tonight's darkness he would be ashamed of in tomorrow's light! He doesn't have to worry about who is around because he is not going to speak any bad words anytime. Why? He is genuinely good inside because the Lord Jesus Christ has made a difference in his life.

When that centurion beheld the life of Jesus and how He lived and how He treated people and how He died, he burst out in praise toward Jesus. The more you look at Jesus, the more you understand that here indeed was a marvelous man.

"Old Faithful" the geyser has not been off more than thirty seconds from its regular eruption cycle since the first time it ever erupted. That is why visitors can be told exactly when to come see Old Faithful spurting water up into the air.

It just so happens that the geological strata under that geyser is so formed that it has no other choice than to erupt at regular intervals. When enough water has seeped into the geological formations beneath that geyser, and is then heated beyond the boiling point by the molten rock below, it has no other choice than to erupt in a display of steam and superheated water. The very nature of it makes it faithful.

Just like Old Faithful, this ought to happen in your life. By your commitment, you are going to be a certain way—Christlike in all you do. That is how God wants you to be. The reason Jesus did what He did was because He was what He was. He was a good man. That is why Luke recorded in Luke 23:47 that the centurion testified concerning Jesus, "Certainly this was a righteous man."

II. The Royalty of Christ

Not only did the centurion see the righteousness of Christ, he also saw the royalty of Christ. I believe the centurion said what he did because of the apparent God-likeness of Christ.

In the Greek New Testament there is no article, *the*, in this phrase: "Truly this was the Son of God" (Matt. 27:54). What the centurion actually said was, "Truly this was Son of God."

Grammatically, this is called a genitive of quality. Every time the New Testament uses this grammatical structure, it refers to the fact that it is a descriptive phrase and not a description of ancestry.

For example, James and John were called "sons of thunder." Those who did the works of the devil were called the "sons of Belial." Others were called the "children of wrath."

I have had women comment to me, "Well, I'll tell you one thing about that boy: he is definitely the son of his father!" By that they meant the boy is just like his dad.

The centurion was not describing the Deity of Christ in respect to His ancestry. He merely meant it was obvious that Jesus was different, and if anyone on this earth had God as his Father, it had to be this man who was dying on the Cross. Jesus is definitely the Son of His Father. So, there is no article.

What the centurion really said was: "Truly this righteous man is Son of God." He did not say "the Son of God" or "a Son of God," but "Son of God!"

When I was in Israel on one occasion, I went to the Hebrew University in Jerusalem. I asked a rabbi why he would not accept the Lord Jesus as the Messiah. I implored, "What problem do you have with Jesus?" I had asked several rabbis that question, and I wanted to hear his answer.

The rabbi said, "Frankly, we see too much humanity." "Tell me about it," I asked. He said, "Well, we don't believe that if God really became incarnate on earth He would have human emotions."

"For instance?"

He answered, "Jesus got angry."

"That's right," I said.

"Jesus wept. He was emotional."

"That's right."

"Jesus got tired."

"That's right,"

I inquired, "But how do you account for the supernatural? How do you account for the miracles? Have you been able to explain those away?"

I thought his answer was interesting. "Well, frankly, we have trouble at that point." Although I did not say it to him, I thought to myself, *You are exactly right!*

You cannot look at Jesus without understanding that He was and is God.

Please remember the background of the Roman centurion. He was raised in the Roman tradition. He was instructed concerning the Roman gods, two of whom, Jupiter and Mercury, were the subject of a typical story taught to every Roman child. The story was this: Jupiter and Mercury one day were on a trip. They went to a village disguised as human beings. Nobody would let them in. Finally Bauclis and Philymon allowed them to enter their home. So Jupiter and Mercury disguised as human beings entered the home of Bauclis and Philymon.

While they were there they became so appreciative of being welcomed by Bauclis and Philymon that when the night's rest was over, Jupiter and Mercury took them to a high mountain peak. They said "Watch!" as Jupiter snapped his finger. All of a sudden water began to rise in the valley of that village.

Soon, water was over the top of every house, and the valley became nothing but a lake. The house which Bauclis and Philymon owned had become an ornate castle that jutted above the water.

Now that is the kind of garbage and legendary saga this intelligent centurion had been fed since he was a little boy. But when he compared all of those pagan, heathenistic ideas of religion to what he had seen in Jesus, he knew there was a difference.

My friend, examine religion, the laws of legend, the myth, religious saga, religious literature. When you do, you will be impressed that this world has been taught much superstition and nonsense that contains no truth and no substance.

Then you look at the life of Jesus Christ, and you will have to exclaim, "Son of God." The centurion was convinced that the Lord Jesus was someone different.

What need do you have in your life today? If you have a need, Son of God can take care of it.

Gaze at the example of the Cross. Jesus was submissive —He was the Son of God and was submissive as an example. He had to be willing to endure pain. This centurion became convinced first of all because of the obvious goodness of the man Christ. Second, because of His apparent God-likeness, He appeared to be like God, and indeed He was!

III. The Response of Heaven

Not only did this centurion marvel at the righteousness of Christ, he also saw the response of heaven. He became convinced that Jesus was the Son of God because of the response of heaven to this cruel treatment of Jesus.

This centurion undoubtedly had seen hundreds of people executed. That was a part of a centurion's assignment. He had seen crucifixion upon crucifixion and never had he seen nature respond to an execution.

Yet when Jesus was crucified, all of a sudden from noon until three o'clock, it was pitch dark, as if it were midnight. People were frightened for their lives. Some began to beat upon their breasts and return to their homes in terror. There was a pitch-black, cave-like darkness upon the earth.

Then the Bible records that after three hours of darkness there was an earthquake. One time in California, I was awakened by a noise, only to find the light fixtures moving around. I had never experienced such a sensation. People later told me at the conference that there had been some minor earthquake tremors that night. The centurion heard Jesus cry out, "Father, into Thy hands I commend My Spirit!" Then the Bible states that He "gave up the ghost." The earth began to quake and rocks were split.

One commentator had an intriguing idea about this. He believed that every rock on earth began to crack. Beneath the feet of that centurion rocks of every size and shape began literally to break open. The Rock of Ages would not break, but all of the other rocks would!

The rocks of the mountains began to crack, and people began to fall into the crevices.

I can imagine, as that Roman soldier looked around to see what was happening, suddenly he may have heard a mighty sound as the veil of the Temple was torn asunder. The Bible records that at the moment of the death of Jesus, they tore, as if giant hands from heaven had ripped the curtain which separated people from the Holy of Holies. It was ripped from top to bottom.

Surely he thought, *That's all that is going to happen.* Then suddenly, dirt began to fly through the air as if someone were shooting it from below. The Bible says the graves were opened, and the saints of the ages began to come out of their graves and to walk in Jerusalem. Many people saw them.

If you had viewed all of that, you would believe that God was trying to speak. When that Roman soldier saw all of that—the darkness, the earthquake, the rocks splitting, the veil of the Temple rent in twain, the graves opening, and the people being resurrected—he began to realize that there was only one conclusion: this is the Son of God!

God is a loving and patient God. But please realize that patience is not pardon. While God may be patient with you now, there will come a day when there will be no more patience. There is no sin like that of rejecting the Lord Jesus in your heart.

When I was a little boy one of my best friends had a drunkard for a father. He was too bad to be called an "alcoholic"—he was a drunkard. Almost on a daily basis he would beat his wife. She was submissive and gracious, yet when you looked at her, it would appear she had the weight of the world on her face.

Her face was drawn, and the lines on it were heavy. Her skin was rough, for she had gone through life at a difficult pace. She could become as docile at a little lamb while her wicked husband was beating her. She came in one day, and that man was on top of her boy, beating him with a stick from the yard. He was hitting the boy in the face, and blood was pouring from one of his eyes.

That woman impulsively and decisively did the only thing she thought to do. She reached toward the drainboard at the kitchen sink, grabbed a butcher knife, and began to slash the body of her husband. The man survived those wounds. When they asked her how she could do that, she replied, "That man can do anything to me, but he had better never touch my son again!"

If you want God against you, you mess around with Jesus. If you want all of heaven's power against you and against your family, you simply turn your back on Jesus. You crucify Jesus in your heart—you crucify Jesus in your life—you start putting Jesus upon the cross of your compromise and mediocrity. You put Jesus on the cross of your unconcern. Then watch out! God will not take it.

You say, "But I thought the sin that God could not forgive was the sin of blaspheming the Holy Ghost." That's right, but do you know what that is?

Suppose Western Union brought me a telegram that read, "The President of the United States desires your presence tomorrow." Then suppose I took that telegram, tore it up, spit on it, and threw it away. Do you think Western Union would be offended? Of course not! My insult would not be against Western Union but against the President of the United States. I did not reject Western Union. I rejected the President's invitation.

When you blaspheme the Holy Spirit, you do not reject

the Holy Spirit—you reject Jesus. Jesus said in John 6:44: "No man can come to me, except the Father which hath sent me draw him." The Holy Spirit is the member of the Trinity who draws men to Christ.

When you are in a crusade, a revival meeting, or another worship service, the Holy Spirit is reaching out at you trying to bring you to repentance and to give up some sin. He calls you to be saved and to give your life to Christ.

Suppose you stand there like a statue unmoved, unemotional, with no burden in your heart, with no concern in your spirit. The Holy Spirit is wooing you and trying to reach you, but you do not respond. Your attitude is one of "I don't care!" God interprets that as a rejection of His Son.

I have thought about all the crimes that have been committed in this world: the atrocities of war, child molestation, pornography, rape, murder, fornication, adultery, and all the rest. Those thousands upon thousands of crimes, yet even an adulterer or a homosexual who repents can go to heaven; even an atheist who repents can go to heaven; even a man who murdered 10,000 people, who repents, can go to heaven. Even a man who would rape a little child could go to heaven if he repents.

Even those two homosexuals who murdered four people in an Oklahoma bank could go to heaven if they would repent. The grossest, most unmentionable crimes ever committed against humanity by those guttersnipes, those low-life people of perverted taste, can be forgiven if the perpetrators would repent and be saved. Even they can go to heaven!

You may be the finest-looking executive in this world or the cleanest housewife that ever lived, but you are going to die and go to hell if you reject Jesus! The one crime God cannot stand is for you to mistreat His Son.

The centurion saw heaven's response to what the world

did to Jesus. God declared, "No more! No more!" That was heaven's response.

IV. The Witness of His Heart

The centurion saw the righteousness of Christ, the royalty of Christ, and the response of heaven. There is a final reason why he could say, "Truly this is Son of God!" He gazed at the witness of his own heart.

I have considerable material in my background and in my study to present apologetics for the faith. I could give you reasons that would scratch the back of your intellectual reasoning on why Jesus is the Messiah. I could read to you the works of Josephus, and you would be impressed with Josephus's evaluation of Christ. I could go on with historians and with intellectual rationale to make you believe that Jesus indeed is the Son of God. However, all of that is inconsequential.

If I were to ask you, "Why are you a Christian?" you would not give me an intellectual reason. I have never asked anyone that question and received some kind of academic answer.

People usually give the same reason that this centurion did. He cried, "Truly this is the Son of God!" When he really looked into the face of Jesus, he had a thirst that was quenched, a hunger that was satisfied, and a longing that was filled. It was the witness of his heart. I can imagine how that soldier, who was an object of unbelievable criticism time and again, found such love there from the Lord Jesus.

I spent an unenjoyable day recently, but I needed to do it. In our crusade at Houston, I met a brilliant judge who invited me down to his courtroom. He said, "I want to show you something." I sat in a spectator's chair for about half a day and watched person after person as they would come to the bench.

The judge would talk to the state prosecutor, and he would talk to the defense lawyer—then he would sentence that person. The judge had compassion, but many times he was limited by the law.

Afterwards we went, of all places, to the evidence room in that Houston courthouse. It made me sick. They showed me the high school picture of a beautiful girl who began smoking marijuana. She had a man who supplied her with the marijuana. One day she refused to increase her clientele for marijuana. He met her at a place where they were to swap marijuana for money, and he beat her to a pulp with a rusty pipe. Her face was swollen and red as if it had been burned.

Then I saw a studio picture of a two-year-old boy who wore a sailor uniform with the little flap for a collar. Then I was shown a photograph of him after a sadist had used a cigarette lighter to burn the inside of his lip. They had also inserted hot rods into his body.

I looked at what criminals had done to some policemen. It broke my heart. I begged, "Judge, I cannot look at another picture."

Then that judge shut the door and shook his head, "Preacher, behind that door is the evidence of the wickedness of man. Society has no answer." He was right! He continued, "I can send them to school. We are now doing many work projects. But I tell them all when I get them alone that the only hope is Jesus Christ!"

I realize we cannot preach Jesus in our schools like we can at church, but if we could, we would have better schools. We would have better government if we could preach Jesus in the state legislatures and in the halls of the U.S. Congress. What a better world we could have!

People will never have the deepest needs of their hearts met, until they meet Jesus!

Tradition has it that the centurion was, indeed, Cornelius. I do not know. Yet I do wonder about the journey of that man. I hope you have been convinced to confess as he did, "This is the Son of God." I must tell you this: the only hope for you and your family and this society is for Jesus to come first in all things. Put Him first and testify with the centurion, "Truly this was the Son of God!"

Then act upon the confession now!

11

Nothing but the Blood

And almost all things are by the law purged with blood; and without shedding of blood is no remission. It was therefore necessary that the patterns of things in the heavens should be purified with these; but the heavenly things themselves with better sacrifices than these. For Christ is not entered into the holy places made with hands, which are the figures of the true; but into heaven itself, now to appear in the presence of God for us: Nor yet that he should offer himself often, as the high priest entereth into the holy place every year with blood of others; For then must he often have suffered since the foundation of the world; but now once in the end of the world hath he appeared to put away sin by the sacrifice of himself. And as it is appointed unto men once to die, but after this the judgment; So Christ was once offered to bear the sins of many; and unto them that look for him shall he appear the second time without sin unto salvation (Heb. 9:22-27).

Several years ago, I was in Flint, Michigan for a crusade. Shortly before we arrived, there had been a fire in a tenement house. Several lives were lost. On the fifth floor of that house was a father who was trying to lead his family to the fire escape.

Several people were running up and down the halls. A

few people from other floors had come to that floor in order to help people evacuate before they would be asphyxiated by the smoke or burned by the flames.

The father had lined up his family so they could climb out of the window onto the fire escape. He told his children to wait by the window while he helped his wife and little infant out. As they went down the fire escape he returned for another and then another.

The last one to leave was a fifteen-year-old girl, but she could not be found when it was her time. The father had seen her a moment before, but now she was not there. Thinking that maybe the girl had been overcome by smoke, he frantically searched for her.

In the process of hunting his daughter, his hands, his face, and many parts of his body were severly burned. The man was rushed to the hospital unconscious because of his injuries.

They later discovered that the girl and a man had jumped from a window, and both were discovered dead on the other side of that tenement house. The authorities imagined that the man believed another window had a fire escape, and that he and the young girl had tried to step out of the window, falling to their deaths.

The newspaper in Detroit reported that the father had been burned beyond recognition. His hands were twisted; the skin was tight and taunt; his face was burned, and swollen; he could not see out of his eyes since they had swollen shut.

As I read that, I thought how tragic that was—a father maimed for life while he was searching for a daughter who was already dead!

As I stare at humanity which has turned its back on Christ, I see people listening to another voice which is calling, "This way! Here is the way of escape!" Humanity has turned against the very One who can give it escape from sudden doom and unquestionable tragedy and destruction.

It is a tragedy that, as far as many people are concerned, the scars of Christ, the riven side, and the crown of thorns were wasted. So were the nails in His hands and feet and His shed blood. They have gone out of other windows only to their imminent death. What a heartache!

There is only one voice to whom you must listen, the voice of Christ. There is only one way of salvation, and that is the way of the blood.

A bloodless religion will never transport you to heaven. A bloodless religion will never usher you into the presence of God. A bloodless religion can never settle your sin problem. "What can wash away my sin? Nothing but the Blood of Jesus!"

That young woman listened to the wrong voice and made a wrong exit to her death. Perhaps you have listened to wrong voices, and your future is one of ever-present doom and everlasting destruction.

As we consider this subject, the blood of Jesus, we are going to examine four areas of biblical thought.

I. Confidence in Prayer

First of all, nothing but the blood of Jesus can give you confidence in prayer. Let the Moslem try to pray, and he cannot, for there is no one who will hear. Let the Hindu pray, let the Buddhist pray—again, there is no one to hear. Unless you go through the blood that was offered on the Cross, you have no access to the Father.

The Tabernacle in the wilderness, which God told Moses and the children of Israel to build, was a beautiful picture of this tremendous truth. Surrounded by the Outer Court, the Tabernacle itself contained the Holy Place and the Holy of Holies.

Inside of the Holy of Holies was the Ark of the Covenant, the only item of furniture placed therein. The Ark of the Covenant was constructed out of acacia wood and covered over with a layer of pure gold. The acacia wood is a picture of the flesh of Jesus and the gold, a picture of His Deity.

On top of the Ark of the Convenant was a solid slab of gold, known as the Mercy Seat upon which sat two cherubim facing each other and gazing down at the Mercy Seat. Inside of the Ark of the Covenant were three items: Aaron's rod which budded, a pot of manna from the wilderness wanderings, and the unbroken stone tablets of the Law.

Why was the Law encased within the gold? Consider the symbolism of the sacrifice. The high priest would slay the lamb and bring a basin of its blood through the Holy Place and into the Holy of Holies. He would then sprinkle that blood upon the Mercy Seat. The Law of Moses, which man could not adequately obey, was under the Mercy Seat inside of the Ark of the Covenant.

When God would look down upon the Law, He would not see the Law, but a seat of mercy covered with the blood. When God looks upon you and me, He sees that we are incapable of obeying the Law. He also sees the Blood of Jesus covering the Law!

The High Priest would wear on the hem of his garment. little golden bells alternating with pomegranates. The people of Israel would stand outside of the Tabernacle and listen for the sound of the bells.

If the high priest did something improper in the Holy of Holies, the Bible says that God would strike him dead. When the people would hear the ringing of the bells, they knew the priest was alive.

If the priest could not live, then the people would have no access to God at all. Thus they would gather around the Tabernacle, and they would listen intently on the Day of

Atonement for the ringing of the bells and the rattling of the seeds. When the people heard that, they knew that indeed their sins would be atoned for. Their prayers went to God by the propitiating, vicarious work of that priest in the Holy of Holies.

When Jesus died on the Cross, that veil in the Temple that separated the people from the Holy of Holies was split from the top to the bottom.

There is a most interesting phrase in Hebrews 10:20, "By a new and living way, which he hath consecrated for us, through the veil, that is to say, his flesh." His flesh is the veil.

As Jesus died, and His veil—His flesh—was torn and split, out came the blood. When the blood came out in death, not only His veil—His flesh—split in twain, but also the Veil of the Temple. No longer would the hight priest have to struggle to reach the Holy of Holies.

Revelation 1:5-6 says: "Unto Him that loves us, and washed us from our sins in His own blood, and hath made us kings and priests unto God and His Father . . . ."

When I read those words I know that you do not need Bailey Smith to get to God. You do not need a Catholic priest to get to God. You do not need anyone but Jesus to get you to God—not even a mom, a dad, a son, a daughter, or a spiritual friend.

You ought to rejoice in the fact that you can go directly to God all by yourself through the blood of Jesus. Thank God that it was not the blood of just any lamb—it was the blood of The Lamb of God.

David Brainerd was a devoted missionary to the American Indians. What a Christian example he set under such unbelievable circumstances. He had an interpreter who deceived him, often misquoting him to the Indians. Even though he was a young man, he had tuberculosis and constant problems with his lungs.

He would be out in the snow sometimes in drifts up to his chest, and he would begin to cough. He would spit out clots of blood until the snow around him turned red. People would ask Brainerd, "How can you continue your work? How can you go on?" He had only one answer: "The blood is on the Mercy Seat!"

He meant: "I go to the Indians. I am willing to spit up blood, to know deprivation. When I preach and do my missionary work, I have access to God. I can pray, and He will meet my needs. My resources are from Him. I can get help from Him because I can, at any moment, go right to God." God called him home at the age of twenty-nine. He literally burnt out for Jesus.

Nothing but the blood of Jesus can give you confidence in prayer. You do not have to worry if God is off somewhere listening to others or if He is preoccupied with some heavenly, majestic activity.

The blood was shed on Calvary and washes away your sins. Because the blood opened up the veil of the Holy of Holies, you have access directly to God. Now you can say, "Thank God! There is nothing between me and my God" Thank God for the confidence we can have in prayer.

I was witnessing one day to a man in an Arkansas town. I asked him if he wanted to go to heaven. He said, "Sure, I think I will because I'm just as good as those people up at the church."

I asked, "Do you believe the Bible teaches that bad people go to hell and good people go to Heaven?" He answered "Sure." I came back, "No, it really does not teach that. What the Bible teaches is that born-again people go to heaven and lost people go to hell."

I asked him, "What do you think they're doing in heaven?" "Well, they're all being good," he replied. I said, "That's right. They are; they don't have any choice." I asked, "What else do you think they're doing in heaven?"

He replied, "Well, I think my momma used to say that they're singing in heaven." I agreed, "That's right."

So I asked him, "Do you think you're going to heaven because you're good?" He answered, "I told you I'm about as good as those people up at that Baptist Church." I wanted to be brutal and say, "Yes, and you're about as bad too," but I didn't tell him that.

I inquired, "What do you think they're singing in heaven?" Then I quoted that song from Revelation 1, "Unto him that loved us, and washed us from our sins in his own blood and hath made us kings and priests unto God." I asked again "Can you sing that song?"

He dropped his head and said, "Preacher, I guess I can't sing that song." I inquired, "Do you have any song at all you could sing in heaven?" He said, "No, Sir." Soon, though, he had a song when he invited Christ into his heart!

One day in another little Arkansas town, the telephone rang. The call came from the courthouse: "Brother Smith, come quickly. A twenty-one-year-old man has been electrocuted. He and his wife had moved here for awhile from Little Rock. They live in a little apartment while he's been working here to refurbish this courthouse. One wire fell across another, and the young man is dead. His wife just can't cope."

I went and tried to help her. Finally, I suggested, "Why don't you just pray?" I have never seen such a look of horror on anyone's face. She moaned, "I can't." I said, "Yes, you can." She said, "No, Preacher, I'm telling you the truth, I can't pray!"

So I asked her, "Why can't you pray?" She explained, "I rejected Jesus a long time ago. I'm not saved. God wouldn't hear my prayer."

I said, "You're exactly right. God won't hear your prayer. But I'll tell you one thing you can do: You can get into a condition where God will hear your prayer, if you will give your heart to Jesus."

In a short time that grieving woman, who less than an hour before had lost her husband, began to pray. As she invited Jesus into her heart, I saw that burden lifted from her shoulders. I saw a new zest about her.

As the blood of Jesus Christ cleansed her from all unrighteousness, and the door of prayer was opened to her, she began to pray, asking God to comfort her and her children.

The blood of Jesus Christ has opened up the Holy of Holies—not unto a priest but unto every person who will come to Christ. Mr. Justice could not enter heaven, and Mr. Mercy could not enter heaven. Then all of a sudden, Jesus came and said to Justice, "Move over! I am taking mercy into heaven!"

What a glorious truth! Because of the blood of Jesus, you can pray confidently and gloriously.

Ty Cobb was one of America's greatest baseball players. He played in 3,033 games—more than any other major league player. He scored more runs (2,244), made more hits (4,191) until Pete Rose came along, stole more bases (892), and finished with a higher lifetime batting average (.367) than any other major leaguer.

He led the American League in batting twelve times—nine in a row. Three times his batting average was .400 or better, and it was .300 or more for 23 straight years. But the Cobb record that baseball historians probably talked about most was the 96 bases he stole in 1915, a record finally broken by Lou Brock.

On July 17, 1961, a preacher came to visit Ty Cobb and told him how to be born again. Cobb looked up from his deathbed and said, "You're not telling me that a whole life of sin can be done away with by a deathbed repentance, are you?" The preacher said, "No, Mr. Cobb, I'm not telling you that deathbed repentance can do away with a lifetime of sin, but I am telling you that the blood of Jesus can!"

At that moment Ty Cobb invited Jesus into his life. As the preacher was leaving his hospital room, Cobb said, "Now, tell all of my friends that I am soory I did this in the bottom of the ninth. I should have done it in the top of the first!"

Aren't you grateful for the access we have to God through the blood of Jesus? Nothing but the blood of Jesus can give you confidence in prayer.

II. Assurance of Forgiveness

Not only can you have confidence in prayer, you can have assurance of forgiveness. Nothing but the blood of Jesus can give you assurance of forgiveness. Christ died on purpose for your sin.

Years ago I bought a book by Albert Schweitzer entitled *The Quest for the Historical Jesus*. I should not have bought it, and I strongly recommend that you do not buy it either.

In his book, Schweitzer wrote that Jesus came to this earth believing He would inherit the apocalyptic kingdom. That is, Schweitzer stated that Jesus literally believed the Kingdom of Heaven would become the Kingdom on earth. When that did not happen, Jesus—because of His mistaken ideas—became a dejected, disillusioned, discouraged prophet who died as a lonely failure.

Jesus was not a martyr! Nor was Jesus a criminal who was caught in an act of rebellion!

Who was Jesus? He was the Paschal Lamb chosen before the foundation of the world. The scars upon the brow of Jesus and upon His hands and feet are still there.

He did not come and die because He was caught in a crime.

Jesus came on a dying mission in the first place. Even before the foundation of the world it was ordained that Jesus would die in your place. Before Jesus was born the angel of the Lord told Joseph: "Thou shalt call his name JESUS: for he shall save his people from their sins." He came to die in your place.

I have found seven covenants in the Scriptures.

Genesis 6:18 describes the Covenant of Safety that God made with Noah. Genesis 17:7-9 records the Covenant of Blessing or Fruitfulness that God made with Abraham and his descendants forever. This is an unconditional, unending covenant.

There is the Covenant of Rest regarding the Sabbath, which is recorded in Exodus 31:16. Numbers 25:12 describes the Covenant of Peace. The Covenant of the Law is found in Deuteronomy 9:9.

The Covenant of Preservation, which is found in Numbers 18:19, is really called the Covenant of Salt in the Scriptures. This Covenant deals with the preservation of the promises of God.

Hebrews 8:8 says, "For finding fault with them, he saith, Behold, the days come, saith the Lord, when I will make a new covenant with the house of Israel and with the house of Judah." This is the Covenant of Blood.

Someone recently asked me what the "INRI." on a Catholic cross means. Should you go into a Catholic Church and look at a crucifix, at the top of the vertical beam of the Cross will be found these four letters: INRI.

The inscription is in Latin. The "I" is for *IESUS*, the Latin word for Jesus. The "N" stands for *NAZARENUS*, The "R" is for *REX*, and the "I" is for *IUDAEORUM*.

IESUS NAZARENUS REX IUDAEORUM literally means "Jesus of Nazareth, King of the Jews." As you think about it, that inscription is an interesting saying to have on a Cross which was a stumbling block to the Jews.

Why is INRI—those Latin letters for those four Latin words—still there? It is still there because God is not through with the Jews. God is not through with Israel because He is in covenant with them. He has a plan for them, and it is the Covenant of the Blood.

We read in Hebrews 8:8, "Behold . . . I will make a new covenant." Scripture teaches that one day when Christ comes, and the Antichrist has been revealed to be a fraud, the Jews will look up and see the One whom they have pierced, and they will repent of their sins.

Paul says in Romans 11:26, " . . . all Israel shall be saved." That is going to come when Israel realizes that without the shedding of blood there is no forgiveness of sin. There is nothing but the blood—be it for Jew or be it for Gentile. Nothing but the blood can provide assurance of the forgiveness of sin. Thank God for that prophetic truth.

III. Power in Daily Living

Nothing but the blood of Jesus can provide you power in daily living. Let me mention four areas in which you can have power in daily living.

A. The Blood Will Frustrate the Power of Demons

"Now, Pastor, you are an educated man. Surely, you don't believe in demons!" I most assuredly do! I even believe in educated demons—I have met a few!

Certainly, I believe in the power of demons. Notice what Revelation 12:11 says: "And they overcame him" [Satan] by the blood of the Lamb, and by the word of their testimony."

Many days of my life I have felt the attacks of the forces below. Many times! Even recently, I have felt them. I do not preach much on demons. I would rather preach on the sufficiency of Jesus, rather than the insufficiency of the demons. The demons are not sufficient to destroy you because you have a greater power within you than without you.

However, they can oppress you unless you are willing to avail yourself of that power. One great truth about the blood of Jesus in daily living is that you can say, "Jesus, I claim your blood over my children today. I claim your blood on this business. I claim your blood on my life, on my habits. Jesus, I need power to deal with this matter."

I would not think of living a day unless sometime during that day, I have marshaled the forces of the power of the blood. There is power in the blood of Jesus. Demons cannot overcome the shed blood of Jesus Christ. There is power in daily living over demonic attacks.

B.   The Blood Is the Path to Peace

Colossians 1:20 reminds us of that truth. The Apostle John wrote in I John 1:7, "But if we walk in the light, as he is in the light, we have fellowship one with another, and the blood of Jesus Christ his Son cleanseth us from all sin."

C.   The Blood Is the Way of Communion

Paul clearly reminds us of that in I Corinthians. Why do we take the Lord's Supper? Why do we take the blood? It is the symbol of our day-by-day communion with the Lord.

D.   The Blood Enables You to Love People

It enables you to get along with people day by day. Every time I see someone, I am reminded that Jesus has died for that person.

Someone once remarked, "Pastor, your problem is that

you try to give everyone all of your time. You just don't discriminate between who is good and who is not good." I asked, "Is that bad?" They said, "Sure, it's bad, because some people just don't need or deserve your time!"

I said, "It's amazing to me that I've never been able to discriminate against anyone, because everyone is someone that Jesus died for."

The next time you start to have prejudice, or you have a problem with a spouse or a child or a brother or a sister, remember they are those whom Jesus loved enough to shed His Blood for.

If we could see everyone as someone for whom Christ died, what a difference it would make. For some, it is wasted because they have not availed themselves of it. Nevertheless, Jesus died for them.

IV. A Home in Heaven

Finally, nothing but the blood of Jesus will secure you a home in heaven. Do you remember what God said to the Hebrew children as they were making preparations for the first Passover? They were given explicit instructions concerning their safety while the angel of the Lord moved throughout the land of Egypt during the visitation of the tenth plague upon the Egyptians.

God told every family among the Israelites to take a year-old male lamb without blemish and to slay it. The blood was to be collected in a basin. They were then to take a bunch of hyssop, dip it into the blood that was in the basis, and strike it upon the lintel and upon the left and right door posts.

When the Death Angel passed over he would look down upon the lintel and the door posts. He would not see the people inside each Hebrew home in Goshen; rather he would see the blood.

God promised, "When I see the blood, I will pass over

you." Indeed, He did! But death came to the firstborn in every home that had no blood.

God also instructed all of the Hebrew children, "None of you shall go out at the door of his house until the morning." When you are a child of God, you must stay under the blood of Jesus Christ until the morning of your resurrection. What a morning that is going to be when we go to be with God.

You say, "Now, Preacher, do you believe in a literal heaven?" I believe in a literal heaven because I believe in a literal God and a literal Jesus.

You say, "Do you believe in the streets of gold?" Let me use a Greek word to answer: "Shoot, yeah, I do! I believe in the streets of gold."

"Do you believe there are going to be gates of pearl?" There are going to be gates of pearl. That does not mean they are going to be made out of aluminum with a pearl every now and then. Each gate of pearl is going to be one big pearl with a gate right through the middle of it!

Why is it a pearl? As you know, a pearl begins as a little grain of grit that lodged itself inside of an oyster shell and has irritated the oyster. The oyster oozed out a milky substance around the grain of sand to prevent the irritation. The oyster coated it with layer after layer. Finally, that milky substance covering the grain of sand hardened and became a pearl. It became something of value.

The pearl represents suffering. The only reason you and I can ever make it to heaven is because of the suffering of the Lord Jesus Christ on the Cross.

The Book of Revelation describes the great power of all those who are against God. There is the mighty Antichrist. There is the force of the false prophet who works miracles. The Bible talks about the "Great Whore"—the apostate church.

Then the Bible speaks about Satan as he opens up the

gates of hell for all of the demonic forces to come out. Can you believe it? Then God talks about the bear—I believe Soviet Russia—that powerful enemy of Israel and all that is good.

Here you have the bear, the false prophet, the Antichrist, Satan, and the apostate. If I were God, I would have written, "And God took an atom bomb, and God took machine guns, and God took missiles, and totally annihilated them all."

However, I want you to see what God really is going to do. How does God meet the mighty Antichrist? How does He meet the false prophet? How does He meet the apostate church? What does God do when the devil opens up the forces of hell and lets the scorpions, and the locusts, and all of the demons come out to plague mankind?

God took a Lamb! A Lamb! A little, bitty Lamb! The name that is used most in Revelation in reference to Jesus is Lamb!

Of all the beings I would have chosen in response to that evil, it would not have been a Lamb. Yet, that is what God chose. Oh, the power of the shed blood of the Lamb.

Look at how often the Apostle John refers to the Lamb in the Book of Revelation:

> And I beheld, and, lo, in the midst of the throne and of the four beasts, and in the midst of the elders, stood a Lamb as it had been slain, having seven horns and seven eyes, which are the seven Spirits of God sent forth into all the earth (5:6).

> And when he had taken the book, the four beasts and four and twenty elders fell down before the Lamb, having every one of them harps, and golden vials full of odours, which are the prayers of saints (5:8).

> Saying with a loud voice, Worthy is the Lamb that was slain to receive power, and riches, and wisdom, and strength, and honour, and glory, and blessing (5:12).

And I saw when the Lamb opened one of the seals, and I heard, as it were the noise of thunder, one of the four beasts saying, come and see (6:1).

And said to the mountains and rocks, Fall on us, and hide us from the face of him that sitteth on the throne, and from the wrath of the Lamb (6:16).

After this I beheld, and, lo, a great multitude, which no man could number, of all nations, and kindreds, and people, and tongues, stood before the throne, and before the Lamb, clothed with white robes, and palms in their hands (7:9).

And one of the elders answered, saying unto me, What are these which are arrayed in white robes? and whence came they? And I said unto him, Sir, thou knowest, And he said to me, These are they which came out of great tribulation, and have washed their robes, and made them white in the blood of the Lamb (7:13-14).

For the Lamb which is in the midst of the throne shall feed them, and shall lead them unto living fountains of waters: and God shall wipe away all tears from their eyes (7:17).

And they overcame him by the blood of the Lamb, and by the word of their testimony; and they loved not their lives unto the death (12:11).

And I looked, and, lo, a Lamb stood on the mount Sion, and with him an hundred forty and four thousand, having his Father's name written in their foreheads (14:1).

These are they which were not defiled with women; for they are virgins. These are they which follow the Lamb whithersoever he goeth. These were redeemed from among men, being the firstfruits unto God and to the Lamb (14:4).

The same shall drink of the wine of the wrath of God, which is poured out without mixture into the cup of his indignation; and he shall be tormented with fire and brimstone in the presence of the holy angels, and in the presence of the Lamb (14:10).

And they sing the song of Moses the servant of God, and the song of the Lamb, saying, Great and marvellous are thy works,

Lord God Almighty; just and true are thy ways, thou King of saints (15:3).

These shall make war with the Lamb, and the Lamb shall overcome them: for he is Lord of lords, and King of kings; and they that are with him are called, and chosen, and faithful (17:14).

Let us be glad and rejoice, and give honour to him: for the marriage of the Lamb is come, and his wife hath made herself ready. And to her was granted that she should be arrayed in fine linen, clean and white: for the fine linen is the righteousness of saints. And he saith unto me, Write, Blessed are they which are called unto the marriage supper of the Lamb. And he saith unto me, These are the true sayings of God (19:7-9).

And he was clothed with a vesture dipped in blood; and his name is called The Word of God. And the armies which were in heaven followed him upon white horses, clothed in fine linen, white and clean. And out of his mouth goeth a sharp sword, that with it he should smite the nations; and he shall rule them with a rod of iron; and he treadeth the winepress of the fierceness and wrath of Almighty God. And he hath on his vesture and on his thigh a name written, KING OF KINGS, AND LORD OF LORDS (19:13-16).

And the wall of the city had twelve foundations, and in them the names of the twelve apostles of the Lamb (21:14).

And I saw no temple therein; for the Lord God Almighty and the Lamb are the temple of it. And the city had no need of the sun, neither of the moon, to shine in it: for the glory of God did lighten it, and the Lamb is the light thereof (21:22-23).

And there shall in no wise enter it any thing that defileth, neither whatsoever worketh abomination, or maketh a lie: but they which are written in the Lamb's book of Life (21:27).

And he shewed me a pure river of water of life, clear as crystal, proceeding out of the throne of God and of the Lamb (22:1).

And there shall be no more curse; but the throne of God and of the Lamb shall be in it; and his servants shall serve him (22:3).

It is no wonder that John the Baptist, when he saw the

Messiah coming, could say, "Behold the Lamb of God, which taketh away the sin of the world."

The shed blood is from the Lamb of God. When we are talking about the Antichrist, the Devil, the false prophets, all the demons of hell, and all the powers of darkness, I want you to know: you do not need to come against them with your reasoning.

You do not need to come against them with your intellect, your rationality, your church budget, your committee meetings.

We come against the powers of Satan with a little Lamb who shed His Blood. All of the powers of darkness cannot destroy that Lamb. When the Rock of Gibraltar is nothing but dust and when the Alps have come to nought but deep, sunken valleys in the ocean floor, the blood of the Lamb will still be powerful enough to save the world! God bless the Lamb of God!

My friend, one day that Lamb is going to come. Are you going to be ready? Are you washed in the blood of the Lamb?

12

Bearing the Cross

And there went great multitudes with him: and he turned, and said unto them. If any man come to me, and hate not his father, and mother, and wife, and children, and brethren, and sisters, yea, and his own life also, he cannot be my disciple. And whosoever doth not bear his cross, and come after me, cannot be my disciple. For which of you, intending to build a tower, sitteth not down first, and counteth the cost, whether he have sufficient to finish it? Lest haply, after he hath laid the foundation, and is not able to finish it, all that behold it begin to mock him, Saying, This man began to build, and was not able to finish. Or what king, going to make war against another king, sitteth not down first, and consulteth whether he be able with ten thousand to meet him that cometh against him with twenty thousand? Or else, while the other is yet a great way off, he sendeth an ambassage, and desireth conditions of peace. So likewise, whosoever he be of you that forsaketh not all that he hath, he cannot be my disciple. Salt is good: but if the salt have lost his savour, wherewith shall it be seasoned? It is neither fit for the land, nor yet for the dunghill; but men cast it out. He that hath ears to hear, let him hear (Luke 14:23-25).

Years ago, I was in Amarillo, Texas, standing on a street corner while waiting for a bus. I looked in a bookstore window, and a sign caught my attention which read, "Crosses Half Price." That sign reminded me that many people see Christianity as a bargain-basement deal.

One theologian spoke about "cheap grace." Baptists love to talk about being saved once and for all—"Once saved, always saved." I believe that, and you believe that. Yet many times we have used that as an opportunity to float in the pool of God's grace, instead of being all that God wants us to be when once we have been born again.

The Bible strongly relates to us: if we expect to wear the Crown, we have to bear the Cross. When Paul stood before Agrippa in Acts 26, he explained the wonderful reasons why he had been born again. "King, I wish everyone could be like I am." Then he added an interesting phrase, "except for these chains."

Paul's willingness to be in bonds, in shipwrecks, in stripes, in beatings, and in many persecutions made him the man he was. One day, Paul will be able to wear the Crown of Righteousness because he did not refuse to wear the Cross of Discipleship and to bear the Cross of Commitment.

Someone mailed me a clipping I thought was lamentable. It was an advertisement in a tabloid. It says, "Your own Holy Cross, blessed in Jerusalem just for you. Each Holy Cross is prayed over in the actual tomb of Jesus just for you. We guarantee it or your money back. Yes! Yes! Please rush to me my blessed olivewood cross." (Probably it was made from an ash in Arkansas.)

"Made in Jerusalem to enhance the goodness and prosperity in your life. Owning this blessed Holy Cross can help you gain fulfillment of the many promises Jesus made to you: happiness, good health, comfort, peace, prosperity, wealth, and more." Then it becomes worse. The world always wants a marked-down cross.

Have you noticed the popularity of the television

preaching which says: if you do certain things, you will always have new tires on your car? You will have gold, diamonds, and prosperous blessings? It is amazing that when Jesus spoke to the people, He did not try to draw a crowd.

The Bible states in Luke 14:25 that when He turned around He saw the multitude. He tried to separate the weak from the strong, the halfhearted from the whole-hearted, the cold from the hot, and He said, "Look, I do not necessarily want a great multitude following Me. I am going to tell you what it means to follow Me."

In Luke 9:57 a certain man said to Jesus, "Lord, I want to follow You. I want to be one of Your followers." Jesus said, "Foxes have holes and birds of the air have nests, but the Son of man hath not where to lay his head."

Jesus often gave people words of discouragement, not words of enticement. He did not want people merely to join up in the movement called Christianity, He wanted them to know what it meant.

I once heard if you give Americans a membership card, they will join almost anything. That may be so. However, Jesus did not offer you a plastic card that gives you credit anywhere in the department store of faith; He promised you a cross. Not one that is marked down and not one made of olivewood. A cross!

It means more than a symbol on the top of a steeple. It is more than jewelry you wear around your neck. I have always thought it enigmatic, at the best, to see a tennis celebrity who is cursing the referee while wearing a gold cross around his neck.

When Jesus talked about a cross, He was not referring to your husband losing his job. He was not alluding to the fact that your mother-in-law came to live with you. Nor was He thinking about the fact that you have gone through bad times.

The cross meant one thing to listeners, as they heard Him say in Luke 14:27, "Whosoever doth not bear his cross, and come after me, cannot be my disciple." Had Jesus been born in the twentieth century, instead of the first, perhaps He never would have made this statement— the reason being that today executions are not carried out on a cross.

If Jesus had lived in modern times, maybe He would have said this, "He who is not willing to pick up his electric chair and follow Me cannot be my disciple." What people thought of when they heard the word "cross" was a means of execution. Jesus was saying, "If you are not willing to pick up your electric chair and follow Me, I do not want you to be one of Mine. You must be willing to be executed in order to be a follower of Mine."

These are strong, unyielding, almost strident words, as you hear Jesus say, "Whosoever is not willing to hate his father, and mother, children, and brother and sisters, bear his cross, and give up all he has, cannot be My disciple."

Once a man prayed, "Lord, I want to have the desire of the Apostle Paul to be crucified with Christ. I want stigmata in my hands and feet. I want scars on my forehead like Jesus bore. Give me a riven side like Jesus had. I want to be willing to be crucified." Then he heard the most astounding Voice from heaven which said, "You can never be crucified with Jesus because there is a scar you do not have!"

He replied, "But Master, I do not understand. I have told You I want to be crucified with Christ. What do You mean that can't happen to me because there is a scar I don't have?" The Voice continued, "You remember that before Jesus died on the Cross, He carried that Cross. You must have a scar *on your shoulder* before you can have scars in your hands and feet!"

Will you ever be able to testify with the Apostle Paul,

"I am crucified with Christ: nevertheless I live; yet not I, but Christ liveth in me."

In this chapter we are going to concern ourselves with your cross and mine. I see in this passage four aspects of bearing the Cross of the Lord Jesus Christ.

I. Limitless Love

Jesus emphasized the Cross to the multitude in order to weed out the insincere ones, like Gideon narrowed his band down to 300 fighting men.

It is not how big the dog is in the fight, but how big the fight is in the dog. Gideon knew that a long time ago; Jesus was aware of that. He knew it is not so much how vast the multitude but how sincere each person is.

Jesus challenged this multitude, "If you are going to be one of Mine, you have to hate your dad and mother." That got their attention! I have never heard of a church having a "Hate-Your-Mother Week" or a "Despise-Your-Dad Day."

The original Greek word translated "hate" in this verse is *miseō,* which means "to bitterly hate or detest." So the Greek did not help me a bit, because it states that you have to bitterly hate and detest your dad and mother in order to be a follower of Jesus Christ.

How do you cope with that, knowing the Bible tells us to be loyal to our parents, parents to be loyal to their children, husbands and wives to be loyal and submissive one to another?

Some commentators noted that this is an ancient instrument of rhetorical comparison. That means Jesus was saying, "Love your mom, love your dad, love your brother and sister. But, compared to how much you love Me, it ought to appear that you hate everyone else in comparison to your love for Me." If only we could love Jesus that much!

At what point would your love for Jesus stop. Would you
say, "Preacher, if a Communist soldier put a pistol to my
head and said, 'Deny the Lord,' I would just say, 'Pull the
trigger' "? Is that right?

Have you noticed that Jesus appeared to 500 at one
time after His resurrection? When it was safe and secure,
He had 500 faithful followers. However, do you remember that there were only 120 in the upper room when
they were understanding the demands of commitment?

In Luke 10 there were only seventy when He sent them
out two by two. Do you remember when He asked for
people to follow Him daily that there were only twelve?
Certainly you remember when He was on the Cross there
was only one disciple present! It went from 500 to 120 to
seventy to twelve to one. Although these events are out
of chronological sequence, they do illustrate the fact that
the greater the demands of discipleship, the fewer there
are who are willing to pay the price required in bearing
the Cross. The demands of discipleship are stern!

You say, "Brother Bailey, I cannot hate my mom and
dad!" That is right. You cannot and you should not hate
your parents. The emphasis of the Bible is love.

Listen to the words of Jesus in Matthew 5:46, "For if ye
love them which love you, what reward have ye? Do not
even the publicans the same?"

Consider the words of the Apostle Paul in 1 Corinthians
13:13, "And now abideth faith, hope, love, these three;
but the greatest of these is love." The Apostle John said
in 1 John 4:8, "He that loveth not knoweth not God; for
God is love."

If there is any great recapitulating theme through the
Bible, it is love, love, love! God does not want you to hate.
He wants you to love. But He stresses that when people
compare how much they love football or an avocation or

their jobs to how much they love Him, it ought to appear to be hatred.

Not long ago, I noticed that one of the charcoals in our grill had fallen out on the ground as I was cooking. All of the charcoals were white with heat inside the grill, but the charcoal lying on the patio looked cool. I reached down, picked it up, and put it right back where it was. It only looked cool, friend! I had a little scar for awhile because of that charcoal.

What I discovered was that in the darkness of the grill with the lid almost shut, the coals looked white hot. However, in the radiance of that great ball of fire in the sky, the coal looked cold.

God is saying this: "I want your love for your mother and your dad and for other things to be warm and vibrant. However, when you compare that love to the radiance of the love you have for Me, it ought to appear to be hatred. I am to be Number One in your life!"

Number One in your life is, indeed, that which you give first place in your life. I have had people say, "Preacher, Jesus is my Savior, but He is not first." There is a real problem then, because He will assume only one place—first!

Whatever has first place in your life is your lord. So Jesus cannot be Lord and Savior of your life if He is not "Numero Uno."

If you are going to bear the cross of the Lord Jesus Christ, you must have limitless love, love without the limits of selfishness, wrong priorities, fear of others' opinions, littleness, negative spirit, and compromise.

Can you imagine what we could do for God if we had such undaunted love? Limitless love! God is saying, "I must be Number One. That is the only place I am willing to be."

While I was pastor of First Baptist Church of Hobbs,

New Mexico, I had a young man frantically wanting to see me one morning. He confessed, "Brother Bailey, I just had to tell you this. Do you remember the girl I used to date before I went off to Army basic at Ft. Benning, Georgia? Do you recall that you told me not to date her?"

"Yes, I remember," was my response.

He went on: "My mom and dad were not too pleased with it either, but I kept dating her. I moved to Georgia, and I fell in love with a beautiful Christian girl. As you know, we have been married now almost a year. Brother Bailey, two days ago my wife went back to Georgia to visit her folks, and I was here in Hobbs by myself.

"Brother Bailey, my old girl friend came by. She knew my wife was away. Pastor, she made herself very available to me, and for one fleeting moment there was that male desire. I was telling some guys at coffee this morning about it, and they said, 'You're stupid. Man, here you had an opportunity. Look what you gave up!'

"But, Brother Bailey, when that old girl friend was there, I reached back and I got my wallet. I took the picture of my wife out, and I said, 'This is the one I love, and she is the only one I love. Since I gave my life to her, I just don't have room for any other affections. I appreciate your coming by, but you really need to leave, because I want you to see that she is the woman I love and I have given my life to.' "

Sometimes after we are saved, Satan comes and reminds us of what we used to do, where we used to go, and what our loyalties once were. Satan whispers, "What you really need to do is this: Get back into that just a little bit." When that happens, we need to pick up the Word of God and say, "Satan, the God of this Bible is the first love of my life. This is where my loyalty is. This is where my devotion is. This is where my commitment is." The Bible promises that if you will trust the Lord and resist the devil, the devil will flee from you. "My Jesus, I love Thee, I know Thou art mine. For Thee, all the follies of sin I resign."

II. Faithful Following

If you are going to bear the Cross of the Lord Jesus Christ, there must not only be limitless love, but also a faithful following. Jesus spoke about that commitment in Luke 14:28-30. "For which of you, intending to build a tower, sitteth not down first, and counteth the cost, whether he has sufficient to finish it? Lest haply, after he hath laid the foundation, and is not able to finish it, all that behold it began to mock him, Saying, This man began to build, and was not able to finish."

Many people come to the brink of blessing and miss it. Hebrews 10:35-39 goes:

> Cast not away therefore your confidence, which hath great recompense of reward. For ye have need of patience, that, after you have done the will of God, ye might receive the promise. For yet a little while, and he that shall come will come, and will not tarry. Now the just shall live by faith: but if any man draw back, my soul shall have no pleasure in him. But we are not of them who draw back unto perdition; but of them that believe to the saving of the soul.

God wants us to be faithful every day in every way. It does not matter what the circumstances are. It does not matter what the commitment has to be. One might remark, "Well, how much do we have to visit, Brother Bailey? How much do we have to do about witnessing? How much money do we have to give? Do we have to give 10 percent? Do we have to give 20 percent?"

A Christian does not even need to ask that. What he does need to ask is, "Whatever it takes." If God needs 100 percent, then that is what I must give Him. Sometimes my loyalty to Christ may not have to be as demanding as it is on other occasions. If God wants 10 percent here, I gladly give it. But if the next month, God's work needs 75 percent, I gladly give it. It really does not matter how much.

When I gave my life to Jesus, my commitment was: "God, whatever it takes to get the job done. That is what I am willing to do. Whatever it takes!" You must remember that if your "faith" fizzles before the finish, then it was a failure from the first. God wants us to continue in commitment.

Do you remember watching, as I do, on the national news after the Beirut bombing as General Paul Kelly leaned over the young Marine who had his eyes blinded by that explosion which killed almost 250 young Americans? The Marine had a tracheotomy in his throat and could not speak or see. When General Kelly leaned over, the Marine reached up and touched the four stars on his shoulder.

Two days later the Marine had a birthday, and the General brought those four stars back and gave them to the young Marine. He said, "Son, we are so proud of you for what you have given for your nation." The young man could not speak, but he made a motion with his hand. He wanted to write a note.

They gave him a pad and a pencil, and he wrote the two words that are on the insignia of the United States Marine Corps. Those Latin words, also the title of a John Phillip Sousa march, are the commitment of that valiant group of men—*Semper Fidelis. Semper Fidelis* translated into English means "Always Faithful." Those were the only two words from that young Marine. Blinded and barely hanging onto life itself, he wrote to that general: "*Semper Fidelis*—Always faithful." We must say to our Lord, "Lord, we do not care about the cost. Always faithful—right to the very end!"

III. Intense Involvement

To bear the Cross of the Lord Jesus Christ properly, there must be limitless love, a faithful following, and an instense involvement.

Luke 14:27 speaks of involvement. "Whosoever doth not bear his cross, and come after me, cannot be my disciple." The key word here is "his."

Every person who is born-again has a cross. If we looked at your cross today, what would it look like? Would it be a little bit worn because you have been carrying it? Or I wonder if your cross would have cobwebs. Would your cross be a little bit musty? Jesus challenges us, "Get involved."

Words are cheap, promises are cheap, pledges are cheap, intentions are cheap. Jesus tells us, "I want you to be willing to bear *your* cross and to come after Me in order to be My disciple." Knowing the perfect will of God means being a crossbearer.

George W. Truett wrote years ago, "To know the will of God is the greatest knowledge, to find the will of God is the greatest discovery, and to do the will of God is the greatest achievement." The will of God for every Christian is that we become involved.

If you were to write the Christian biography of many people, it would be this: "They got saved. They got baptized. They sat in a folding chair for forty years and in a pew forty years. They died and went to heaven and have been sitting ever since!" God does not want you to be a spectator all of your life as a Christian.

He wants you to be visiting, soul-winning, teaching, singing in the choir, on the finance committee, personnel committee, property committee, going on mission trips. God wants you to be picking up that cross and bearing it!

When a man went up on the stage after a performance

of the traveling Passion Play and, as a joke, put his shoulder under the cross and tried to lift it, he could not do so. He commented to the famous actor who had played the person of Christ for so many years, "I thought that the cross would be made out of balsa wood. I thought it would be made out of cardboard and painted. I had no idea that it was literally made out of heavy wood."

The actor observed, "That cross, as far as we know, weighs the same amount as did the cross upon which Jesus died." The man was puzzled. "Why? This is only a play." The actor responded, "I have learned that I could never really look like Jesus unless I bear the same weight He bore!"

You might suffer and not be saved but you cannot be saved without suffering. There is going to be some suffering. The Bible explains that the servant is not better than his Master, and the Master gave His life in suffering! There is an intensity of involvement for those who are saved.

When they come to you and ask, "Can you serve?"— *Yes!* "Can you work?"—*Yes!* "Can you do this?"—*Yes!* Why? Because you settled that long ago when you answered "Yes" to the Lordship of Jesus Christ. It was all settled long ago.

IV. Sacrificial Service

To bear the Cross means not only limitless love, a faithful following, and an intense involvement, but also sacrificial service. Jesus warned in Luke 14:33, "Whosoever he be of you that forsaketh not all that he hath, he cannot be my disciple."

You implore, "Brother Bailey, everything? All?" Yes! All of your ambitions, all of your goals, all of your habits, all of your schedules. You protest, "I would hate to give up everything." Do you realize that if you gave up everything you have, you would still be richer than most of the world? Did you know that last year two billion adults had an annual income of less than $650?

God has been good to Americans, yet we are a bunch of spoiled brats. Jesus is saying, "Unless you are willing to forsake all you have, then you cannot be my disciples." God has been so good to us, so abundant toward us. If we are not obedient to Him, 20,000 people will starve to death this day!

You may choose to eat out today. You will be able to make a choice whether you want fish, beef, or pork. You will be able to make that choice, and yet there will be thousands of people who wish they could have what you and I may leave on our plates.

You ought to go home and thank God for dirty dishes. One man said, "Boy, we would have a lot to be thankful for at our house!" There are thousands and thousands of people who will never have that. God has been so good to us.

When Billy Graham was in Oklahoma City for his 1983 Crusade, we were honored for him to speak at our church family that Sunday morning. He told us about that Korean woman who never missed a service in his Crusade in Seoul, Korea. She lived three miles from the crusade site with her husband who was a quadriplegic. She would bend down at her home and pick up her husband. Even though she weighed only 90 pounds, she would put her husband on her shoulders. Then that little lady would walk three miles to the Billy Graham Crusade. She would put her husband down, and they would listen with intensity to Graham's preaching. When it was over, she would stoop down, put her husband on her shoulders, go back home, and put her husband back in bed. And they would be there the next night. Why? Because she wanted to be. She was willing to bear the cross.

A Christian must do "whatever" it requires to get the

job done for Jesus. Are you willing to have limitless love? Are you willing to be a faithful follower? Are you willing to have to have an intense involvement? Are you willing to make a sacrificial service unto the living Lord? If you are, there is nothing in this world or in hell itself that can stop you!